A NOVEL WAY TO DIE

COZY MYSTERY BOOKSHOP SERIES #2

TAMRA BAUMANN

Text copyright © 2020 by Tamra Baumann . All rights reserved.

ISBN: 978-1-947591-11-0

Published by Tamra Baumann

Cover Art by The Cover Vault

Printed in the United States of America

A Novel Way To Die

CHAPTER 1

$\mathcal{M}$y eyelids must be superglued together. As hard as I try, I can't seem to pry them open. I'd really like to confirm I'm still alive.

Antiseptic hangs heavy in the air. Luckily, I doubt that's how the afterlife smells. I hope I'm in our tiny hospital/clinic.

But I'm getting way ahead of myself here. A long chain of events has happened that brought me to wherever I am right now. This story really starts a few days ago in my recently inherited bookstore, Cloaks, Daggers, and Croissants. We were getting ready for a big book signing when I asked a simple question of my newly discovered adopted fifteen-year-old sister Brittany...

"Are we ready for our guest author?"

"All set," Brittany replies without taking her eyes off the phone in her hand.

She has a propensity for dressing all in black and rolling her eyes, but she's a good kid. I already care deeply for her.

Brittany finally meets my gaze. "And the queen of crime's list of demands has been fulfilled as well. Down to the lavender plug-in air fresheners and her fifty-buck-a-bottle hand sanitizer. If I ever get famous, Sawyer, please remind me not to be a jerk like Angelica Kane."

"How about I remind you now?" I toss her a rag. "The bookshelves still need dusting. Nothing like hard work to keep an aspiring celebrity humble."

Before Brittany can achieve all 360 degrees of her eye roll, my best buddy Renee, who is tall, olive-skinned, dark-haired, and gorgeous, walks through the front door of the bookshop. She's wearing a sexy red jumpsuit with strappy black sandals and bearing ice cream from her shop, the Daily Scoop.

"Sawyer and Brittany," Renee says, "I need your help. I'm trying out a new flavor. It's called blackened-heart cherry. In honor of your guest author who'll be signing books in the blood she probably sucked from innocent children. And other people's boyfriends!"

I laugh despite my best efforts to hold it back. "Hold a grudge much?"

Renee scoffs. "I already told you I don't care that you're hosting the signing. Angelica and Zach grew up here too. Zach, the gold digger, can have his rotten-author meal ticket.

Me? I'm going to bask in my good fortune that he ran off with her instead of ruining my life by marrying me." Renee sets three dark red sundaes oozing with thick chocolate sauce on the counter and digs into hers first. "Ice cream is sweeter and more comforting than any man I've ever met."

"Angelica Kane's husband, Zach?" Brittany asks.

"The one and only," I answer. "Zach used to be engaged to Renee until Angelica lured him away with her fame and fortune right after college." It left Renee hurting and resolved never to have another serious relationship again. I think she will when she meets the right guy, and believe me, she has no shortage of men in her life.

Brittany's eyes widen as she pounces on her ice cream. "You got dumped at the altar too? Like Sawyer did?"

If one more person brings that up...I'm over that. And I am trying to mend fences with Dylan Cooper, who's now the sheriff of our small town.

Renee shakes her head. "Lucky for me, Zach hadn't even bought the real ring yet. He gave me his class ring and said he'd replace it as soon as he had the money. But he never came by any money until he married Angelica, so that sort of put an end to the whole engagement-to-me situation. Not that you won't find the perfect soul mate and live happily ever after, Brittany." Renee glances at me. "Sorry, Sawyer. I forgot we're supposed to be molding Brittany's young mind with positivity and good karma."

Brittany shrugs. "My mother dumped me for a man too, so whatever."

That breaks my heart, so I slip an arm around Brittany's shoulders. "Your mom left you in my mother's capable hands because yours knew she wasn't cut out to be a parent. We should give her credit for that. And now I have another sister. It's all a big win-win the way I look at it."

Brittany glances at Renee, and they share a "let's humor the poor optimist" look that I'll just ignore. Because, well—I *am* an optimist. What can I say? "Cooper agrees with me at least, don't you, buddy?"

My adorable mini goldendoodle with a white chin, who my mother bought for me before she died, raises his head. Cooper has been snoozing in the summer sunshine on a comfy couch in the front window of the bookshop. He thinks it's his personal throne. My mom's cozy mystery bookstore has themed reading nooks scattered about. I might have to rename the Sherlock Holmes Baker Street Retreat into Cooper's Doggy Den.

When his tail starts wagging and he jumps from the couch, I assume he's coming to support me. Until he heads for the window and sits up tall like he's expecting his best buddy. A glance toward the front door confirms he is.

Sheriff Dylan Cooper, my former cold-footed fiancé, ambles inside. "Hi, ladies. Sawyer, can I speak with you, please?" He tilts his dark-haired head toward the door as he squats to pet my traitorous mini doodle. Mom named the dog after Dylan in an attempt from the grave to remind me to take my former fiancé back one day.

Today isn't that day.

Dylan and I are becoming friends again, but I'm keeping my guard up. My heart still has the bruises he left there eight years ago.

Dylan gives my dog a generous rub along with one of his signature movie-star-worthy grins. "Hey there, Cooper. How's it going, buddy?"

Cooper wags his goofy tail and promptly rolls on his back, demanding an indulgent belly rub. Maybe my dog is taking "being pushy" lessons from our guest author, Angelica Kane. She'd called last week and said she was bringing hundreds of her fans with her to Sunset Cove, our tiny Northern California coastal town, since she had to visit her mother anyway. Her enthusiasm for the event had been underwhelming, to say the least. Unlike her list of demands. Those have been daunting and ever changing. I have to give Brittany points for her restraint when dealing with such a spoiled diva. "Brittany, will you please watch the shop for a few while I have a chat with Dylan?"

Renee sends me a smirk as she licks ice cream from her spoon. She finds the recent competition for my attention between Dylan and my mom's sexy lawyer, Gage, amusing. I find it confusing. I'm just an average-looking brunette who hates the gym and loves to cook. And to eat, of course.

After Brittany nods her consent to watch the store between bites, I turn to Dylan and say, "What's up?"

He stands and smiles at me too. "I've been thinking about something."

Before I can ask about what, he takes my arm and leads

me out the front door in that pushy way he has when he's got something big on his mind. I'm not sure he even realizes he does it. Weirdly, I've missed being with a man who's that passionate about how he feels.

We cross the street to the town square and then to a cluster of benches on the far end. He says, "Maybe we should sit."

"Okay." I choose a bench that faces the ocean, hoping the crashing waves against the cliffs below aren't going to be indicative of what tumultuous thing Dylan might have to say.

When Dylan's face tightens with a familiar seriousness, my stomach takes a dive. It's the same way he looked when he listed all the reasons he had to bail on me at the altar. "What is it? Did you figure out who sent that golf ball flying through my shop's window a few weeks ago?" The one that said menacingly, SAWYER GO HOME on it. Or something close. Cooper's drool had made some of the words smear, so it's a bit of a guess.

He shakes his head. "No. No new leads there. This is personal."

Uh-oh. Now my stomach is filled with angry wasps. "How personal?"

"So personal it's going to possibly hurt. Me. Not you." He flops beside me and takes my hand. "I want you to date Gage."

He could've said my hair was on fire and I would have been less shocked. "I don't understand. Why would you want me to date my mother's lawyer?" Not that Gage isn't handsome too. Because he is. And really nice. We've had a few pleasant business dinners recently.

Dylan, blue-eyed and full of muscles and brawn, leans his big khaki-uniformed shoulder next to mine and whispers, "You obviously like him. So, I need you to explore that. I won't be anyone's second choice. And when you finally come to your senses and realize you still love me, we'll talk."

I don't know if I want to punch Dylan or kiss him. Instead, I close my eyes and count to five. "We've talked about this. The day your brother married my sister changed everything. We're stuck with each other every holiday. What if we try again and it doesn't work? Maybe it's best to wait and see how things go. Naturally. Not via your silly science experiment." I mumble under my breath because I can't help it, "And since when do you get to pick who I date?"

"You already picked Gage. Not me." Dylan slips an arm around my shoulders and pulls me close.

I can't say I hate it. He's nice to hug—all muscle and male. "Gage and I are just friends. Maybe I'll find someone to date online. Like Renee does." Actually, I hate that my best friend does that. It doesn't seem safe. But Dylan doesn't need to know that.

Even though he probably does. He knows me better than anyone else.

He slides his finger under my chin and gently tilts my face toward his. "I can see the way you look at Gage. Like he's one of your shiny French cooking pans or something. I hate it, but if he's who you want, then I'll step aside. I want you to be happy, Sawyer."

Oh, man. Now he's gone and made my heart all gooey. I hate that. It makes things ten times more complicated.

I'm just a displaced chef from Chicago trying to get my life in order after my mother left me with a crumbling Victorian house, a failing bookstore, and a trust fund I have to outsmart to finally open the restaurant my mother always wanted me to have. My uncle is trying to take my mother's share of said trust, but I'm invoking a loophole I found. If I can keep the loophole a secret, it will allow me to build the restaurant of my dreams without my uncle knowing. I'm so close and don't know if I can afford a relationship too right now. "I think I might want to live like a nun for a year or so first—man-less, and reflective."

Dylan's grin slowly grows into a mischievous one. "I'd like to test that theory." He moves his mouth a breath from mine and whispers, "But I need your permission first. To kiss you."

Kiss me?

My hormones scream, *Yes, please!* while my brain is shouting, *Don't you dare!*

Unfortunately, hormones are a powerful thing.

Since it's not the worst idea I've heard all day, I close my eyes and kiss him first.

It's like a bomb goes off in my judgey brain, silencing the protests immediately. Kissing Dylan is like coming home on a cold wintry night to a raging fire and a hot cup of cocoa.

Sweet and warming all the way to my toes. His kisses touch me in places… Maybe I'd better keep things G-rated here and lean away.

Luckily, Dylan leans back first. With a self-satisfied grin on his handsome face, he says, "That kiss just made a liar out of you. And I don't think nuns are allowed to lie."

I roll my eyes Brittany style. Mostly because fooling Dylan is impossible. "Fine. I'll date Gage to see if there's anything there. I bet he kisses ten times better than you do, anyway." I peel off Dylan's arm that has wrapped itself around my waist. "Let go before the whole town has us married with two kids."

He quickly moves his arm to his side. "We always said we'd have three."

"Yeah. But I'm older and wiser now. Two kids *plus* a bossy husband will probably be all I can handle. See you later, Sheriff." I stand to leave.

"*I'm* the bossy one?" A low laugh rumbles from Dylan's chest as he stands too. "Who was the one who insisted we go to that restaurant in the city all the time? The one with the candles and the white tablecloths, and with wine no one can pronounce? The place with the hovering waitstaff who scowl when you pick up the wrong fork to eat your fancy snails. Mario's, wasn't it?"

My favorite place. We used to go there to celebrate special occasions. Dylan is good at invoking good memories while pushing my buttons at the same time.

I place my hands firmly on my hips to show him I'm not

taking the bait. "Keep it up, and you won't have to worry about me dating someone else. You'll be too busy solving your own murder." I turn to walk away as Dylan's big hand wraps around my arm to stop me.

"Sawyer, wait. I was kidding. Please. Talk to me. Tell me where I stand here."

The desperation in his voice as he slowly turns me to face him hurts my heart. "I've forgiven you for jilting me." He was confused when he left me and joined the army. And still is in some ways over his parents' bitter divorce and his mother's subsequent death because of it. "But I'm not sure I can risk being hurt like that again. And I do like Gage—as a friend. That's all I know for sure right now."

He slowly nods in understanding. "What I know for sure is I love you. Never stopped. And I'll always regret leaving you. It was the dumbest move I ever made."

"It was." I close my eyes and lean my forehead against his hard chest. "This decision would be so much easier if I hated you for getting cold feet. I've honestly tried to hate you. *Really*, really hard. But I can't."

That low rumble in his chest sounds again. "You're such a sweet talker. It's what I love most about you."

"Very funny." I poke him in the side and lean away. "I've got to get back. Big signing and all. We'll talk later, okay?"

"Yep." He shoves his hands into his khaki pants. "Is Renee okay with seeing Zach again?"

"Unlike me, Renee knows exactly how many ways she'd like to see her ex pay for what he did to her. I think I admire that about her." I smirk so he knows I'm kidding. "I'm serving death-by-chocolate cake at the signing if you'd like to stop by later." I start walking backward toward the store, across the grass, because I like to see him smile. He loves that cake as much as I do.

He lays his hand across his chest. "That you'd make my favorite dessert—despite my *bossy* ways—makes my heart soar."

I don't want to smile, but I can't help it. "Admit it. You're really coming to be sure Renee doesn't hit Zach over the head with something."

"That too. Bye." He smiles and lifts his big hand, watching me until I have to turn around to cross the street.

What am I going to do about Dylan? And Gage? And my new secret restaurant? And my new little sister? I don't know how to be a parent. I'm just learning how to be a good dog mom, much less a pseudo mother to a fifteen-year-old. Would Dylan or Gage want to deal with my new sibling? Because Brittany and I come as a package deal now. My sister, Megan, the brain surgeon, has her own family in San Francisco. But I can always count on Meg for help and advice. She's the best.

Better to pull a Scarlett O'Hara and think about it all in the morning. I have my first big book signing to pull off. People from nearby San Francisco have called to confirm Angelica will really be in our store this afternoon, so I ordered extra books I hope I can sell.

This signing could make or break the bank this month.

My store's shaky bottom line is riding on the signing's success.

∼

LATER IN THE AFTERNOON, the store is packed with Angelica's fans fawning over her and her handsome husband, Zach, who has been put in charge of charming the ladies waiting in line.

Finger snapping sounds and Angelica's fake singsong voice calls out, "Sawyer? Be a dear and get me some more of that watermelon water, with extra ice. And another of those lovely croissants too, while you're at it."

My mom always had gourmet coffee and croissants delivered to the store every day, free to anyone who stops by, and I've kept the tradition going. But today the crowd has been so large, we've gone through four extra croissant deliveries and three of my death-by-chocolate cakes. I saved a piece of cake for Dylan that I hope will still be there by the time we close.

Brittany's eyes cut my direction. "Yes, Sawyer. *Do* be a dear, won't you?" Brittany can't contain her grin any longer. "Why does she talk like she's British and sixty? Aren't she and Zach like your age? Forty-five or something?"

Brittany knows I'm only thirty-two. She and Dylan apparently went to the same button-pushing school. They both must've graduated top of their class. "Yes. Which means I'm entirely too old to run down the street and get

12

more croissants. You'd better do it," I say in my best British accent.

"You should leave the bad Brit act to your pal over there. Want me to take Cooper home so he doesn't have to be stuck in the stockroom?"

"Yes, please." I feel bad for my poor little dog who is normally everyone's instant best friend. Cooper had sat and held up a paw for a high five when Angelica and Zach had come in. Angelica was on the phone and didn't see him. Zach asked Brittany to remove Cooper immediately because Angelica has allergies. "Make sure he has a rawhide, so he doesn't chew up my new molding in the laundry room."

Brittany nods and takes off to get Cooper. Then she heads for the front door with my dog on his leash.

Dylan is there and holds the door open for my new little family to walk by, then he joins the line near the register where I'm working. He must've finished up his work for the day, because he's dressed in jeans and a white T-shirt that shows off his nice chest and abs. He rarely gets a whole Saturday off, so I'm glad he's taking the afternoon at least.

I smile, and he returns it before I get back to the line of customers waiting to be rung up. "One moment, please, while I get something for Angelica. I'll be right back." I run to the kitchen and pour more watermelon water with extra ice. When I turn around, I nearly run into Angelica's husband. The only thing the same about him from high school is that he's tall. Now he's blond, fake tanned, with bleached teeth, and has had more Botox injections than Angelica. "Hi, Zach."

He hasn't spoken to me since they arrived, instead focusing on pushing Brittany around. He probably still remembers my reaction when he dumped my best pal. It hadn't been very nice.

"Hey, Sawyer. Thanks." He grabs the glass from my hand. "Were you this pretty in high school?"

While I did make an effort today, throwing on my fanciest blue dress and black heels rather than my usual dress slacks and a blouse, I don't tend to stand out in a crowd. People always say I remind them of someone, but they can never remember who. However, I have a snarky side that has been tested all day by our diva author, so I say, "Actually, I was in a terrible car accident and had to have total facial reconstruction a few years ago. I'm surprised you even recognize me."

Zach's eyes go wide in horror before he laughs and slaps a big hand on my shoulder. "Got me again, Sawyer. You and Renee were both the biggest smartas—"

Dylan's loud grunt cuts Zach off.

Zach lifts his chin in greeting toward Dylan and then finishes, "Alecks. Smart Alecks." Zach quickly drains Angelica's glass. "That's amazing. Can I have some more?"

"Sure." I draw a deep breath and tell myself this will be over soon. Then I can lock the doors and count all the money we hopefully made today. I fill two glasses and stick them out. "Will you take a glass to Angelica too, please?"

"You bet." He takes the glasses and asks, "Is Renee still around? I was hoping to see her today."

"I don't know. But you should see what she's done to the shop since her parents retired. She's added amazing baked goods now too. A one-stop shop for everything delicious."

"Really?" Zach shows off his fake white teeth. "I'll have to pop over there before the shop closes. Thanks again." He lifts the glasses like he's toasting me and then wades back into the crowd to deliver his wife her drink.

I shake my head at his arrogance and wonder for the millionth time what Renee ever saw in the guy. Then I go back to my patient customers and get busy ringing up books again.

After another hour, the crowd thins, and the Admiral, who runs our book club each week, finally gets his autographed book. He's grinning as he approaches the counter to pay for it. "Hello, Sailor. Great turnout today."

"It's been amazing." He knows my name is Sawyer, but he rarely uses it. Why I'm the only person he calls Sailor is a mystery I haven't solved yet. But then, the Admiral is his own mystery disguised as either a genius or a man who's losing his marbles one by one. I haven't decided which yet. "Did you get to talk to your nephew?" I glance around, but Zach is nowhere to be found.

The Admiral, tall, white-haired, and always dressed in a cardigan and slacks, blinks at me for a moment before the lightbulb goes on behind his eyeballs. "Technically, he's my late wife's nephew. Not mine. Besides, I never really liked the lad. He thinks he knows more about sailing than I do. Can you imagine that?"

Actually, I can. Zach was always full of himself. I point to the signed book. "I'm surprised you have to buy that. Angelica and Zach must know what a mystery lover you are. Don't they send you free copies?"

The Admiral leans close enough that I can smell the peppermint he's sucking on. "Not since I told Angelica I could tell she wasn't writing her own books anymore. The tone changed along with the technical expertise used in the murders. But don't say anything. Obviously, all these people haven't figured it out yet."

That's super interesting. While it's no crime to hire ghostwriters, I'd never figured Angelica to be the type to let go of enough control to do that. "My lips are sealed." I run my fingers across my mouth like closing a zipper. But now I want to read some of Angelica's prior work to compare it with her new books.

When the last customer finally leaves, I lock the door behind me and lean against the glass to take stock of the day. Brittany left a while ago to let Cooper out of the laundry room at home. Dylan is back and cashing in on the leftover cake that I stashed for him, and Angelica is on the phone whining about her broken nail. She wants her manicurist to drive down from San Francisco to fix it tonight. Maybe her mother has high nail standards or something.

Angelica, who's scary thin and with hair dyed platinum blonde—she's actually a brunette like me—has a face that barely moves due to all the injections as she yells into her phone. She finally hangs up on her caller and then focuses on me. "Sawyer. Where's Zach?" Her fake British accent has suddenly disappeared. Maybe she only does that for her fans?

"I don't know. I haven't seen him for hours. But thanks for today, Angelica. You did me a great favor."

She waves her hand. "It's the least I could do. Your mom was always my biggest fan. Even when I was writing garbage in middle school."

I hadn't known that. "You obviously figured out how to turn that garbage into bestselling words, so congrats." Even if she isn't writing all of them herself anymore.

Angelica isn't listening. She's busy on her phone again this time yelling at her agent about something. All I want to do is go home and soak my tortured feet in a hot bath. Wearing heels all afternoon isn't for the weak of heart.

When Dylan's phone rings, he reluctantly stops eating his cake. He says, "Z, slow down. What did you find in the freezer?"

Z is what we call Zelda, who works for Renee. She's rich, and yet she works in an ice-cream shop. I've still not figured out why.

Dylan hangs up and then calls the paramedics as he jogs toward the door I'm still leaning against.

"What's going on?" I ask.

Dylan whispers in my ear. "Keep Angelica busy until you hear from me. We found Zach. In the walk-in freezer. Head wound. Z thinks he's dead."

Dead? That can't be. He was just here...

Dylan adds, "Have you seen Renee this afternoon? Z said she hasn't talked to her today."

"No. Renee said she might go into the city to shop. Or go for a long run. Or show up here looking fabulous to make Zach pay. She hadn't decided." Then all the blood rushes from my head to my toes when I realize why Dylan is asking about Renee. "There's no way Renee would ever go through with her idle threats against Zach. This has to be an accident of some sort."

Dylan's jaw tightens. "Let's hope."

CHAPTER 2

*D*ylan has gone to the Daily Scoop to check on Zach, and I'm still standing by the bookshop's doors in shock. I pull out my phone and call Renee. I know in the deepest part of my heart, my best pal would never harm a fly, but it couldn't hurt to confirm how she spent her afternoon. Hopefully, she got a massage or spent money in the fancy San Francisco shops she loves so much. It'd give her an ironclad alibi.

When Renee's voicemail answers, I leave a message to call me and then hang up. Renee always calls back right away or texts. I shouldn't have long to wait to hear what she's been up to all afternoon.

Angelica is still on the phone with her agent while she angrily throws her fancy pens and my expensive hand sanitizer into her tote.

I wish Dylan would call me before she hangs up. Tell me what to do. How am I supposed to act natural when Angelica's husband might be dead in a walk-in freezer down the street?

A loud knock sounds on the front door and makes me jump. It's Angelica's brother, so I turn the lock. "Hi, Andy. Come in."

"Hey, Sawyer." Andy, who could be Angelica's twin except he has their original brown hair color, grimaces. "Dylan asked me to take my sister to our mom's house. I'll break the bad news to her. It's hard to believe Zach's dead. I just talked to him a few hours ago."

"Oh. No. So it's true. I'm so sorry, Andy."

He just nods.

I want to ask Andy if Zach had an accident. But it's not the right time for questions.

Andy throws his shoulders back. "I guess I better get this over with." His troubled eyes quickly search the store for his sister. "Dylan said if Renee calls you, don't talk to her about this. Just have her call him."

"I'm on it." I grab my phone. Of course Dylan guessed the first thing I'd do is call my best friend. This time, I send a text with 9-1-1 as the subject line. Hopefully, that'll get her attention.

After I tuck my phone into my dress's pocket, a loud wail of grief sends a stab of sympathy to my heart.

Angelica hugs her brother while shaking her head. "There

has to be a mistake. Are you sure it's Zach? How could he be dead?"

Andy nods and gently leads his sister toward the door, speaking so quietly, I can't make out the words.

Angelica says between sobs, "It's Kate. I just know it. She's tried to destroy my marriage and my business."

I beat them to the door and hold it open for them as Andy says, "Who's Kate?"

Angelica moans, "My former assistant. I fired her two weeks ago. I told Zach it'd be a mistake to hire her, but he never listens to me."

After they leave, I head straight for Renee's ice-cream shop with my heart bleeding for Angelica. My mom's death is still only a few months old, and the pain of losing someone I loved is still sharp in my memory. And my soul.

Jogging in heels is impossible for a person who rarely wears them, so I stop and slip them off. While stuffing my shoes into my purse, I run toward the top of the square. I make a quick right turn into the ice-cream shop, pretending I don't see Mr. Martinez, who is locking up his art gallery next door. It won't be long before the whole town knows about Zach.

As I cross the threshold, a big hand wraps around my arm and stops me. "You can't be in here. Did Renee call you?" Dylan asks.

"Not yet." I grab my shoes and set the other hand on Dylan's shoulder for balance while I slip them onto my feet. "I sent her a text just now. Angelica thinks her former assistant, Kate somebody, might be behind all this." I want Dylan to focus on the real killer, not my best friend.

Dylan's right brow arches. "You know this how?"

"I overheard Angelica telling Andy. And she was talking on the phone to her agent about a replacement."

"How do you know it was her agent?"

"Because her agent, Sheila, only called fifteen times to be sure we have all the accoutrements necessary to make Angelica a happy book signer."

Dylan nods. "Go on."

"Angelica was talking about how she needed someone she can trust this time. Want me to start googling?"

"No." Dylan sucks in a deep breath like he does when he's trying to be patient. "I'm sure I can get Kate Somebody's phone number from Angelica." Dylan lifts his phone to read a text. "Let me know if you hear from Renee. And no discussing details. Just have her call me."

"Okay." Not that I know any details yet.

I glance around the shop decorated like Willy Wonka's personal treasure trove. Zelda, who's a fabulous mix of Jamaican and Puerto Rican heritage, is sitting at one of the small tables wringing her hands. She's in her forties but doesn't look a day over thirty-five. She changes her hair color often, and today it's a sort of purple hue. It's always a bright color to match her Bohemian style that's equally suited for the island life or San Francisco. "Let me check on Z first. She must be traumatized. Then I'll go."

Dylan narrows his eyes at me. He knows I'm going to

snoop around in his case because of Renee. And I'm starting with Z.

He says, "Three minutes, Detective Buttinski. Not a second more."

I give Dylan a thumbs-up and then plop beside Z. "Hi. Are you okay?"

She nods. "First time I've seen a dead body, though. Not a fun way to start my shift."

"Nope." I rub a hand up and down her back. "What happened?"

Z shakes her head. "I showed up for my shift a little before six. Annie was supposed to stay with me until closing, but her arthritis was acting up again, so she left early. We normally work two to a shift, so Raphe had his hands full when I showed up. He offered to cancel his date to help me, but I said he could leave. It's the boy's first date ever, so I told him to get a move on so he wouldn't keep his lady waiting. I figured I could handle the shop on my own for one evening."

I know that Annie stopped to get a book signed before she went home, but I won't mention that to Z. Annie is an avid reader. Maybe she wanted to read in bed while she recovered. "That was nice of you to let Raphe go when you were shorthanded. But how did you find Zach?"

"About ten minutes after Raphe left and all the customers had their ice cream, I noticed we were getting low on mint chip, so I went into the back. That's when I saw Zach, on the floor of the freezer with his head bleeding. I knelt beside him and noticed he had a piece of paper in his hand. His eyes were wide open, staring at nothing. When I realized he was dead, my knees started shaking, and I got sick to my stomach. I turned around and dashed out front to call Dylan before I passed out."

"I'm so sorry you had to see that."

Tears bubble up in her eyes. "I'm just barely holding it together here, Sawyer."

"You're doing better than I did in the same situation. You were smart to call Dylan right away." I'd had a member of my book club die in my store just a few weeks ago too. It's not something you easily forget. "How do you think Zach ended up in the back?"

"I have no idea. Raphe was in a hurry to leave for his date, but still, I can't imagine he'd forget to mention Zach stopping by. Especially after Renee's warning."

"Sawyer!" Dylan calls out from across the little shop. He must be timing me.

"Gotta run." I hug Z and whisper in her ear, "What warning?"

Z's eyes cut Dylan's way before she whispers back, "Yesterday, Renee showed us a picture and said if that scumbag steps one foot into the shop, we were to let her know so she could take care of him. But it gets worse. You know the note in Zach's hand?"

"Yeah?"

"I couldn't read much, but it was an email from Renee with today's date."

Oh boy. That doesn't look good for Renee. Where the heck is she?

DYLAN THROWING me out of the ice-cream shop had been sort of rude, but necessary, I suppose. He likes to do things by the book. Luckily, I don't have a book of rules I have to follow. I'm going to get busy googling Angelica, Kate the assistant, and Zach as soon as I find Renee. And after I get the key to turn in the lock of my home's front door. It's stuck.

Brother. This lock is the newest thing about my crumbling Victorian monstrosity, and it worked fine this morning. One more thing to fix.

The door sweeps open and nearly yanks off my arm. Brittany, dressed in something skimpy I've never seen before, is standing beside Raphe. "Oh. Hi, Sawyer. I was just locking up. We were going out the back."

That would explain why the lock wouldn't turn. But since when does Brittany invite boys over? "What am I missing here? And why are you dressed like that?"

Cooper zips out the door to greet me like he hasn't seen me in a month. His rear end waggles as hard as his tail as he waits for me to pet him. His exuberance never gets old, but I don't have time to return the love because I think I'm about to get my first real test as a parent.

Brittany says, "It's called a date. We're going to the

movies. I didn't think I needed a permission slip from my *sister*." She crosses her arms in defiance—which is an improvement. She needs to cover up all that skin showing across her stomach.

"You're aren't going anywhere dressed like that." I close the front door behind me and tug on Brittany's arm. "Cooper, keep Raphe company. We'll be right back."

Brittany moans, "We'll be late. The movie starts in fifteen minutes!"

Ignoring her protest, I drag Brittany up the stairs to her bedroom. "Since when do you dress like a goth Playboy Bunny?" Who knew there could even be such a thing? A black tank top, shorts, and combat boots.

Brittany sticks out her bottom lip so far, it'd make any two-year-old proud. "Renee said this outfit looked cool."

"My mom didn't leave Renee in charge of your outfits. Unfortunately, you're stuck with me." I open Brittany's closet and start flipping through all the black clothes, grabbing a T-shirt with a band's name on it. "Here. Your favorite. Just slip it over the top."

Brittany grumbles a bit but pulls the T-shirt over her head with no further arguments.

I add some authority to my voice and say, "We're going to talk more about you dating...tomorrow."

"Fine." She tugs the hem down and then lifts her chin. "Satisfied?"

"Yes. Thank you." I should probably say something parental now. "Do we need to talk about boys?"

She crosses her arms. "I learned what *not to do* with them from my mother. You don't have to worry about that too."

"Okay. Good. Did you guys eat yet?"

Brittany's gaze falls to her boots. "We were going to eat at the movies."

Junk food. We've talked about that. But it's Saturday night. The one night I compromise on her bad eating habits. "How about I make you guys a pizza and then I'll disappear? I can't let you go out tonight. It might not be safe."

"Not go out?" Brittany's black-lined lashes blink fast, like she's fighting tears. "You're ruining *everything*, Sawyer!"

Now I feel like a big jerk for making her cry. "It's not my mission to ruin your date. Something bad happened at Renee's shop, and I don't know if whoever did it is still in town. I don't want to risk you guys being hurt."

Brittany's tears miraculously dry up. "Is Renee okay?"

"That's what I'm trying to figure out. She hasn't returned my calls."

"What about Z? And Annie? Did something happen to them?"

The worry in Brittany's eyes makes mine sting with tears. Brittany pretends to be tough and gruff, but underneath, she has a heart of gold. "They're all fine. And please don't say anything to Raphe about it yet. Dylan needs to talk to him first."

Brittany nods. "Okay. But what happened?"

"I'll tell you everything I can after I find Renee." I set my hands on Brittany's shoulders. "Can I trust you guys here alone while I go look for her?"

"I'm fifteen, not two. We're not going to burn the house down cooking pizza."

That's not what I meant, but I don't want to give her any ideas she doesn't already have about kissing boys. "Okay, then." I squeeze her shoulders. "I'm sorry. I really didn't mean to ruin *everything*."

"I know." Brittany sniffs and then wraps her arms around me. "I'm not used to someone worrying about me either. So, we're even." She gives me a hard hug that melts my heart a little before she says, "Go find Renee. I can make pizza. I've watched you make it a million times, Warden."

Probably best to let the warden comment go. "Great. Save me a couple of pieces."

"I'll save you the ones with anchovies and pickles on them." Brittany smirks before turning on her heels and heading for the door.

Luckily, we don't have any anchovies in the house. I can only hope she's kidding about the pickles. "There are lots of healthy veggies in the fridge for toppings."

"Healthy and pizza don't belong in the same sentence," she says as she starts down the stairs.

True. Saturday junk food pass aside, I can't help my proud grin that Brittany must've actually been listening to all my eating-healthy-food lectures since she's come to live with me. She used to eat out of cans when her mother would disappear for long stretches of time.

When Brittany and I reach the foyer, Raphe and Cooper are both patiently waiting for us in the same spots we left them.

Raphe smiles sweetly and says, "That looks great too, Brit."

I think I like this kid. Even if I wish he'd found a pair of jeans with fewer rips to wear on their date. "Hey, Raphe. Did Renee say where she was going this afternoon? She hasn't returned any of my calls."

"No." Raphe slowly peels his eyes off my sister to meet my gaze. "But she forgot her phone by the register. I heard it chime a few times during my shift."

Well, that explains why she hasn't called me. "I'll run by her house, then. You didn't happen to see the guy in the picture she showed you today, did you?"

Raphe shakes his shaggy blond hair. "No. But Annie told me it was Renee's ex. She said Renee dodged a bullet when he ran off. Guess Annie was his English teacher back in the day?"

"She was mine too." I grab my purse I dropped on the floor in my rush to clothe Brittany. "Is the rear door to the ice-cream shop always locked?"

"It locks automatically. We have to put in a code to open it. Like when we leave or take out the trash."

"Did anyone do that today? Take out the trash?" Maybe someone left the door propped open so they wouldn't have to put in the code? And maybe Zach slipped in that way?

"Must've. There wasn't much when I came on at noon."

Raphe frowns like he's thinking. "Renee probably took it out before I got there."

Brittany's brows scrunch. "Why are you giving Raphe the third degree, Sawyer?"

"Sorry. Just curious. I'm done now." I dig out my car keys. Normally, I walk everywhere, but there might be a murderer running loose. "You guys have fun. I'll be back as soon as I can."

Brittany says, "Call when you find Renee. And then feel free to take your time coming home." She slips her hand around Raphe's arm. "Change of plans. I'm a prisoner, evidently, so we have to hang here tonight."

Raphe grins. "That's cool."

I hope that grin is because he's saving the price of movie tickets and not because they'll be alone in the house.

Brittany tugs Raphe down the hall to the kitchen. "What do you like on your pizza?"

He shrugs. "I don't care as long as it's pizza."

Great. I might end up with pickles on my pizza after all.

I kneel to pet my dog. "Keep an eye on them, Coop. And just this once, you have my permission to sit on the living room couch. Between them."

Brittany calls out, "I heard that!"

Good.

I kiss the white spot on top of my dog's head, then whisper, "Do your job, and there'll be an extra rawhide in it for you."

As if Cooper understands, he wags his curled tail and

heads to the kitchen to play referee. Or maybe it's because he heard the fridge open. Either way, I can count on Cooper to bat his eyes and beg for belly rubs to keep Raphe busy.

I close the front door behind me, turn the lock, then pull out my cell to call Dylan. When he answers, I say, "Raphe is at my house with Brittany. They were going on a date, but I asked them to stay in. I assume you haven't talked to him yet about Zach but want to."

"I planned to talk to him next. His parents were going to wait for him outside the theater to bring him home. Is Brittany old enough to date?"

"I don't know. I was going to google it before I have a chat with her in the morning. What do you think?"

"Fifteen seems young. Now. Not when we were fifteen, though."

"That's what I was thinking. Maybe I shouldn't leave them alone while I go out. Is Raphe a suspect?"

"I can't eliminate anyone yet. But the camera footage shows he stayed out front until he left. Where are you going?"

"To find Renee. I'm worried about her. But I'm worried about Brittany too."

"I need a parent present when I talk to Raphe. I'll tell his folks to pick Raphe up at your house now and take him home. That'll put a damper on the date too."

Phew. That makes me feel better. "Perfect. Then I don't have to be the bad guy again tonight. Bye."

"Wait. I've called and texted Renee too. You can stay put. We'll wait to hear from her."

"Raphe told me Renee left her phone at the shop. Gotta run!" I quickly hang up before Dylan can talk me out of looking for Renee.

As I'm tucking my phone away, a million questions occur. Why isn't Renee checking in? She must've figured out she forgot her phone by now. It isn't like her to disappear. She always answers my calls and texts right away.

A sobering thought hits me. What if whoever killed Zach in Renee's shop was really after her? She's dated a lot of guys online. Some a little odd. What if Zach was just in the wrong place at the wrong time? What if Renee is in serious danger?

CHAPTER 3

*R*enee's adorable little yellow house is right on the ocean. She grew up there and bought it and the ice-cream shop from her parents. After they retired, they moved to Hawaii and later divorced. I spent many hours here as a child, consoling Renee while her parents fought downstairs like cats and dogs. Another reason Renee claims she'll never marry. Zach wasn't the only one who hurt her, but I'm one of the few who know that.

Now, after Renee has made the place her own, it's one of my favorite spots to have a glass of wine and watch the waves crash against the shore.

I pull into the driveway and hop out of the old Honda I inherited from my mom. It has a big flower-power decal in the back window I should probably scrape off, but I don't have the heart. Renee's SUV is in the carport, so hopefully, I can stop worrying about her.

After negotiating the wooden front steps, I poke the doorbell. When no one answers, I walk around to the back. Maybe Renee is sitting on the deck overlooking the ocean, where I usually find her.

When I get to the rear, the deck is empty. The curtains are closed on her sliding glass door.

Should I grab the spare key that has always been under the big pot that sits in the corner? She could just have walked to the store for something. But what if Renee is inside the house? Hurt and bleeding. It's my duty as her friend to do a little breaking and entering to be sure everything is okay. Isn't it?

With one hand, I lift the blue ceramic pot that holds what must be a fifty-pound little tree, grunting with the effort, and with my other hand, sift through the dirt underneath. Finally, my fingers land on a bit of metal. Bingo.

I grab the key and then head back the way I came. When I round the corner near the carport, I slam into something soft and furry. My yelp mixes with a loud female "Umph," before we both end up in a heap on the grass beside the driveway.

It's Madge from my store's book club, who's also our police dispatcher. She knits Christmas sweaters and wears them all year no matter the weather. Hence the soft thud as our bodies collided. Today's sweater is red with a green blob on the front that I think is supposed to be the Grinch. Or maybe a Christmas tree. It's hard to tell.

Holding out a hand to help the dark-haired middle-aged woman sit up, I say, "You scared me to death, Madge. What are you doing here?"

"Saw your mom's car. Figured you were here looking for Renee. Thought I could help. Ben, the new deputy, filled me in on the crime details."

More like she heard about Zach and was so curious, she couldn't stand it. But Madge has an inside track at the sheriff's office and is always ready to share, so maybe I'll let her tag along with me.

I hold up the key. "If your best friend tells you where she hides the key to her house, that's like a legal standing invitation to come in whenever, right? It's not like we'd be doing anything wrong if we look around a bit. Would we?"

"Nah." Madge shakes her head as she reaches inside her purse. "But maybe we better have this handy just in case. For protection. What if a killer is lurking in there?" Madge pulls out a gun.

"Whoa there." I hold up both hands like she's sticking me up. "Doesn't jail time like triple if you have a weapon during a break-in?"

"Dylan's not going to arrest you for checking on your friend." Madge shakes her head as she lumbers to a standing position. "You worry too much, Sawyer."

I stand and wipe off the grass from my dress. "At least tell me you have a permit for that."

"Of course I do." Madge winks at me. "Who do you think issues the gun permits at the station?"

Brother. I hope that means she went through the proper training, but maybe I don't want to ask any more questions of my accomplice. The less I know, the better. "Just be sure the safety is on."

Madge waggles the gun near my face. "It is. See?"

I want to live to *see* my thirty-third birthday. "Maybe you should put that back in your purse. Renee had a guy do feng shui inside a few weeks ago. I don't think guns fit into the good yin and yang that's going on now in her house." I'm totally making the yin-and-yang part up. But my mother had been into crystals and chakras and such, so Madge might believe me.

"Fine." Madge shoves her gun back into her purse. "Wouldn't want to throw off anyone's karma or anything. Besides, I've practiced quick drawing it from my purse. I'm pretty fast."

"What a comfort." I stick the toe of my shoe into the crack between the screen door, which has never closed all the way, and the front door. A familiar loud groan sounds as I turn my back to it to hold the screen open.

"Geez," Madge says. "That door would wake the dead. She should have that looked at."

"It's just ancient. And no more talk about death, please. I'm already freaking out." I slip the key into the lock. Touching only the key, so I don't leave prints, I slowly turn the knob and stick my head inside.

"Wait!" Madge grabs my arm to stop me. "If there is a bad guy in there, now he knows we're here too. Because of that screen door. I'm getting my gun."

"But nothing looks out of place." I tiptoe inside and whisper, "Leave the door open behind you, though. In case we have to make a quick escape."

"Good plan." Madge follows close behind with one hand tucked inside her green purse that hangs from her shoulder.

We turn right and into the kitchen. It's been recently remodeled with lots of stainless steel, granite, and has glass-front cupboards.

Madge whispers, "I could never keep my dishes neat enough to have see-through cabinets."

"I could." But then, some might call my kitchen freakishly neat. "Why don't you check the back door. See if it's locked. But don't touch it with your bare hands." Testing the slider is something I should have done earlier when I was on the deck but didn't think to do it.

"I'm the one who reads all the murder mysteries, not you. I know better than to touch anything." Madge shakes her head, pulls her sweater over her hand, and tests the sliding door. "Locked."

"Doors both locked and no signs of a break-in or struggle, so we can probably assume no bad guys are here. Let's keep looking, though. Maybe she left a clue as to where she went."

As we walk out of the kitchen, the front door slams closed with a loud thump, making us both jolt.

"I'm outta here." Madge turns and starts running for the sliding door.

My heart thumps as I turn to follow right behind.

But something isn't right. I stop and look over my shoulder. I don't see anything. Or anyone. "Maybe the wind did that."

Madge skids to a stop and turns around. "Or maybe the bad guy just sneaked out?"

"Nope." I just remembered what was wrong. "We would've heard the screen door."

"True. Moaning Myrtle would've been proud of that screen's groan." Madge lays a hand over her heart. "That nearly killed me."

"Moaning Myrtle?"

"You know?" Madge lifts her hands. "From Harry Potter. That girl who lives in the bathroom. Who would want to live in a bathroom for the rest of their days?"

"That's where the entrance to the chamber was. She guarded it, that's why. Let's keep looking for clues."

"'Kay."

The living room is its typical neat and tidy self, although newly rearranged because of the feng shui, with a comfy blue couch and a matching chair. A closed laptop sits on the coffee table, and the black heels Renee wore earlier are tucked underneath the table. There's a piece of paper next to the computer that catches my eye, so we head that direction.

It's a trail map. Renee often runs or bikes in the woods

outside town. Maybe she found a new trail to explore. I take out my phone and shoot a picture of the map.

Just as I'm tucking my phone away, a creak sounds above our heads, and we both jump again.

"This old house does that all the time," I confirm with as much confidence as I can muster while glancing at the ceiling. "We should look upstairs next."

Madge nods. "You first."

"You're the one with the gun."

"That you won't let me use. Maybe I should stay here by the front door and keep a lookout?"

"For a fast getaway at the first sign of trouble?" I grab her arm and pull her along with me. "You're all in on this now too. We can share a jail cell if we get caught. I hope you don't snore."

"I hope you still know how to use your womanly charms on Dylan. We might need them."

"I thought you said he wouldn't arrest me."

"I've reconsidered. Maybe he's lost interest in you in all the years you were away."

If that smoldering kiss we shared earlier was any indication, I'm pretty sure I still have what it takes to charm the sheriff. However, that thought is wildly inappropriate at the moment, so I'll just push that pleasant memory aside for now. "Let's hurry up so we don't get caught in the first place." I open a closet under the stairs where I know Renee has a softball bat and grab it.

Madge says, "Why the bat? You just said there wasn't a break-in."

"You're so jumpy, you're making me that way too. Can't hurt to both be armed." Shouldering my new weapon, I start up the wooden steps, avoiding the known creaky parts that might alert an intruder that we're here. Just in case I'm wrong, and there is one.

Madge, on the other hand, walks like she's stomping grapes, so I abandon my sneaky ways and jog to the top.

Stopping at the landing to wait for Madge, I glance toward the guest room door on the right that's slightly ajar. Using the bat, I poke the door open. Inside, the bed is made as usual, with nothing out of place. So I opt for Renee's bedroom on the opposite side of the hallway.

Madge is huffing behind me as I creep toward Renee's closed door. Luckily, her bedroom door has one of the long handles instead of a round one. Using my elbow, I press down, and the door swings open.

We both step tentatively inside. I'm hoping with all my might I don't see Renee hurt and bleeding. Luckily, the room is empty. The bathroom door is standing open and looks unoccupied as well.

Madge lets out a low whistle. "This is one sexy boudoir."

It is. Pretty candles, half-burned, sit on the hand-carved nightstands and dressers, silky pillows on her giant bed add a nice touch to the frilly spread, and soft and flowing material billows with gusts of wind from the open windows. Renee's bedroom always smells like flowers and spring.

The red jumpsuit she wore earlier is hanging on the back of her open closet door like she was going to put it back on later.

"Let's look in the bathroom, just to be sure it's really empty," I whisper.

"Statistically, the most dangerous room in the house," Madge whispers back. "Do you know how many times Dylan has had to go to Crystal's rescue in hers? And how many times he's seen her naked?"

"Wait. What?" A sharp pang of jealousy stops me dead in my tracks. Crystal is my nemesis from high school. She's redheaded, curvy, gorgeous, and has always been in love with Dylan. "Why would she need rescuing so often?"

"The door sticks. Especially when she's showering, evidently." Madge grins. "Not that you'd care or anything, right?"

I care a lot, apparently, but Madge doesn't need to know that. "Dylan wants me to date Gage, if you must know. Can we *please* stay focused here?"

"Prickly subject. Got it." Madge salutes. "Staying focused now."

We start walking again, and I go first into the bathroom. Renee converted her old bedroom into a personal spa space. It has a massive shower with multiple jets, a deep tub for soaking, a makeup area, and mirrors everywhere. But still no Renee. I'm relieved and, at the same time, worried now more than ever. "Where could she be?"

Madge is busy examining the shower. "I bet Renee's door

doesn't stick. This is one fancy situation going on here."

I spin around. "I thought you meant the door to Crystal's bathroom sticks. She took her phone in the shower, and then called Dylan when the *shower* door got stuck?" My voice has risen three decibels, so I clear my throat. "And he didn't see right through that?"

"Oh, he sees a lot. Especially of Crystal when that happens. But she didn't take the phone in with her. She called out, and her electronic gadget thing dialed Dylan's number. That voice-command business has saved many a life. I mostly use mine in the kitchen to set timers and tell me the weather."

I'm grumbling under my breath about how Crystal needs to add the station's number rather than Dylan's to her gadget when the screen door's familiar loud groan sounds from downstairs. "Someone's here."

"I'm not going down without a fight." Madge grabs her gun.

She really is a fast draw. "Put that away. It's probably Renee." I hope. But I grip the bat even tighter.

"We're sitting ducks if it's not."

True.

Heavy footsteps on the stairs send my heartbeat into overdrive. "That's not Renee. Maybe we should hide. The closet!" I whisper-scream.

Madge and I run to the closet and close the door behind us. With chests heaving, we both lean forward, straining to hear in the dark. The footsteps are moving closer.

The blood pounding in my ears is making it harder to hear, but the steps seem to disappear into the bathroom.

"Let's make a run for it," Madge says in a voice entirely too loud. "Go!"

Whoever's out there had to have heard Madge, so I fling the door open and start running. Madge's clomping steps are right on my heels when a large arm with a latex glove on its hand slips around my waist and swings me off my feet. The person belonging to the big arm yanks the bat from my hand before my shoes land with a thud on the tile floor of the bathroom. The mirror above the sinks reflects me with disheveled hair and a perturbed sheriff with a gun strapped to his side. Behind him, Madge is sneaking out of Renee's bedroom.

"Not so fast, Madge. You get in here too," Dylan says as he leans the bat against the doorframe and moves aside for her to join me.

Thankfully, Madge has slipped her gun back in her purse before she slides beside me and says, "It's not B&E if you have a key. Show him the key, Sawyer."

"B&E?" Dylan crosses his arms. "What if whoever killed Zach had been here? You could've both been hurt."

"Or." I hold up a finger. "What if Renee had been stuck in her shower and needed help? Oh, wait. You're the one all the women in town are supposed to call when they're naked and wet, aren't you?"

When Dylan's brows arch, it occurs to me that came out

all wrong. "I mean when they're in the shower. *Stuck* in the sho—"

He holds up a hand. "I get it." His eyes narrow in my coconspirator's direction. "But apparently, someone else doesn't. Madge must've forgotten that official police business is none of anyone else's business."

Madge shrugs her yarn-covered shoulders. "Crystal told anyone who'd listen. She said you had to rescue her three times."

My jaw drops. "Three?"

When Dylan glares at Madge, her gaze drops to her tennis shoes. "Okay. The shower rescue only happened once." Her eyes move my way under heavy lids. "Crystal was *allegedly* fully clothed the other two times."

"Enough." Dylan huffs out an exasperated breath. "Did you find anything to help figure out where Renee went?"

"Maybe." Happy to talk about anything other than bathrooms, I pull out my phone and show Dylan the picture of the trail map. "This was by her computer downstairs."

Dylan studies the screen. "Her car's here. Is her bike gone?"

"I don't know. She keeps it in the shed off the deck."

"Then let's go check out the shed. But no more touching things, ladies."

We all troop down the stairs and out the moaning screen door. Dylan stops and holds out his gloved hand. "Key, please. The one contaminated with your fingerprints."

Ignoring his snarky remark, I hand it over.

He locks up the house, while Madge heads for the rear. When he's done, he whispers, "Are you and Madge going to be a pain this whole investigation?"

"Looks that way." I hurry to catch up with Madge before Dylan can expound on his question.

However, Dylan is faster and catches up with me. "Sawyer."

His tone says he's not amused.

I stop and huff out a breath. "What?"

"I need to interview Renee before she hears any details of the crime. Is that clear?"

"Crystal."

"Speaking of Crystal." He wraps an arm companionably around my shoulders as we walk to the rear of the house. "Do we need to talk about the shower thing?"

"Not necessary." I cross my arms and try my best to sound like I'm not affected in the least by the shower story. "I've been with other people too, since we broke up." This is my sneaky way of asking if he and Crystal have ever dated.

"For the record, I've only seen Crystal sort of naked that one time. It sure beat the cat-stuck-in-tree calls I usually get." He squeezes my shoulder, so I know he's pushing my buttons again.

At least she was only *sort of naked*. Not all the way naked. I'm dying to ask the details, but that'll make it look like I'm too curious. "The tough life of a small-town sheriff. Remind me to feel sorry for you later."

Dylan chuckles as we climb the steps to the deck, where

Madge is waiting for us.

She says, "I didn't touch anything."

"That makes one of you." Dylan unlocks the shed door and pushes it open with his left shoulder as his right hand hovers over his gun. Inside, there's the usual gardening stuff, a lawn mower, and rakes hanging on the wall. On the workbench, there's a small sledgehammer, not in its place above the bench. That's obvious because there's only one empty tool outline. Renee's father was fastidious about his tools and putting them back. I remember when he painted all those lines so there'd be no excuses to put the tools away incorrectly.

I turn and check the hooks where Renee's bike usually hangs. They're empty.

A huge wave of relief floods through me. "Looks like she's out riding."

Madge walks over to the tool bench. "Ben said Zach was killed with something round and heavy. Maybe something like this?" She points to the bench. "Is that what I think it is?"

Dylan must've seen whatever she saw first, because he's already got his phone next to his ear. "You ladies need to step out, please."

Madge grabs my arm and leads me outside. "Come on, Sawyer. We should let Dylan do his job."

"What's going on?" I glance over my shoulder. Dylan's not smiling anymore.

Madge answers, "I'm no expert, but that looked like blood spatter on the hammer's handle."

CHAPTER 4

*B*lood spatter?

Sure, Renee would scathe Zach with words or slay him with kindness, but there's no way she'd ever hit anyone with a mini sledgehammer.

As I sit on Renee's back porch and ponder, the summertime sun continues to extinguish itself in the ocean. It won't be long until it's dark. Renee doesn't ride in the dark if she can help it, so maybe she'll be back soon. I glance around to see if Dylan and his men are almost finished.

Ben, the new tall, thin deputy whose shaven head makes him seem older than twenty-nine, is still taking pictures inside the shed. Dylan has gone back inside the house to look for more evidence, so I whisper to Madge, who is sitting beside me on the deck, "What did Ben say about the crime? Every detail. Don't leave any out."

Madge leans closer. "Zach was knocked on the head with a round blunt object. It also looks like he hit his head on the edge of a metal table. Which blow killed him, they won't know until the autopsy comes back. Ben's guess is hitting the sharp edge of the table was the fatal blow. They found lots of prints on things, but they need to eliminate all the employees first. No other physical evidence was found in the freezer except a printed email from Renee sent earlier today. No signs of forced entry either."

That email bothers me. "Why would Zach print out an email? Don't most people just read them on their phones? It's like someone planted that. But why?"

Madge shrugs. "Maybe whoever did this wanted to be sure Dylan looked at Zach's emails. What if the killer is leaving clues? Playing with the police, like, 'I'm going to make this easy for you, and yet you still won't ever find me?'"

"Or..." I lift my index finger. "What if whoever hit Zach didn't mean to kill him? Just hurt him, but didn't plan on him hitting his head when he fell? In a panic, the killer could've missed the paper in Zach's hand?"

"Who knows? But I still can't see Renee hitting anyone." Madge shakes her head.

"I think Renee is being framed. We need to figure out who'd want to do that. That's the key to solving Zach's murder. But first, we need to find Renee."

Dylan's deep voice behind us says, "I've got deputies looking for Renee. You two need to stay out of this, but I know I'm wasting my breath." He flops into the seat beside mine. "You ladies want to grab a quick bite? I'm going to have to pull an all-nighter."

Madge stands and shakes her head. "Norm just texted me in all caps. He's waiting for me to come home to make dinner. You'd think the man would make himself a sandwich, if he were that hungry. See you guys tomorrow." She lifts a hand and then heads for her yellow VW bug parked at the curb out front.

"Bye." I return the wave. "I'll text you when we find Renee."

Madge nods. "I'd appreciate it."

Dylan waits until Madge is gone and then says, "So how about it? Want to grab a burger?"

"I thought you wanted me to have dinners with Gage, not you."

"It's not a date. I want to talk to you while we eat. Kill two birds. I have to get back to the station."

Why that disappoints me a little is hard to pinpoint. "Brittany is supposed to be saving me some pizza. With who knows what for toppings. If you'd like to join me, I have some leftover quiche in the fridge too. Besides, Brittany dealt with Zach more than I did. You'll want to talk to her too."

"Great. Your leftovers are better than anything Jerry serves at the diner anyway." Always the gentleman, he stands and waits for me to go first.

I grab my phone from the table and head down the steps. "Have you guys started looking into Kate, the assistant?"

Dylan sighs. "My deputies all have their assignments. Right now, I'm most concerned about Renee's safety."

I beep my Honda open with the remote. "Me too." Dylan opens my door before he rounds to his and slides in beside me. I ask him, "Do you think someone is setting her up?"

After he's all buckled in, he says, "I think we need to be sure no one else gets hurt while we look at all the evidence." He's answering texts as we pull out of the driveway.

"Agreed." I put my car in gear and consider what we know. "Speaking of people getting hurt, did the interview with Raphe go well? Is it still safe for Brittany to see him?" I can't imagine Raphe has anything to do with this, but better safe than sorry.

"If I said it'd be better to hold off seeing him for a bit, would that take the pressure off? Until you figure out if she should date yet?"

And that's what I like about Dylan. He knows how I think. "It would. I need to talk to my sister and see what she thinks too."

"Then quote me."

"Thank you." As we start up the hill to my house, a thought hits me. "But if I forbid her to date, will that just make her sneak behind my back?"

Dylan chuckles. "We did. Just one more reason your dad never liked me."

"My dad is still mad about losing his deposit from the 'groomless wedding that shall not be named.' Don't expect him to get over that anytime soon."

"I'm not holding my breath." His phone rings, so he takes the call. "Sheriff Cooper."

While he talks to one of his men, I continue the short drive to my house. Our town is so small, it takes precisely three and a half minutes to get to my old Victorian from Renee's house. My mother inherited the house from her parents, and she left it to me. It's a beautiful big home with a remodeled kitchen, wavy glass windows upstairs that have ocean views, and classic lines that make it a grand old gal, but it could use a significant face-lift otherwise. The trust has money I can use to repair any safety issues, but only in small increments or I have to get my controlling uncle's approval. For now, I'm more focused on getting the trust to build a restaurant for a mystery customer my mom's lawyer Gage is handling. Of course, that mystery customer is me. My uncle will blow a gasket when he figures out it's not some celebrity chef from San Francisco like everyone assumed. I'm kind of looking forward to that day. For the moment, I'm keeping my head down and staying as far away from Uncle Frank as I can.

After we pull into the garage, Dylan hangs up, and we head for the kitchen where we're assaulted—in the best possible way—by the unmistakable aroma of sugar cookies baking. It makes my stomach growl. "Wow. Those smell good."

"They do." Dylan heads for the cookies cooling on racks on the island. But first, he's intercepted by an enthusiastic

Cooper, who is batting his long eyelashes at his best friend. Dylan squats to my dog's level. "Hi, buddy."

Once Cooper gets his fill, he flops at my feet and rolls over for a second belly rub. I'm not sure who has whom trained here, but I comply anyway because he's like a little stuffed golden teddy bear and is hard to resist.

Dylan stands to grab a cookie just as Brittany appears from inside my large pantry. "Stop, or I'll shoot." She holds up a pastry bag filled with icing. "Back away from the cookies, and no one gets hurt."

Laughing, Dylan holds up both hands. "Sorry. I thought they were fair game."

I open the fridge and pull out the leftover pizza. "Why aren't you sharing, Brittany?" Thankfully, she's changed into flannel pj pants and a T-shirt.

She points the bag at me. "Because someone ruined my date by calling..." She points the bag at Dylan again. "Him. I'm making these for Raphe to say I'm sorry I live with a snitch. He's so mad at me, he's not returning my texts. Couldn't you have waited until after dinner at least to send his parents for him?"

"Nope." I pull the pizza from a plastic zip bag, and relief fills me. Brittany topped the pie with mushrooms and ham. "Not when there's a murderer on the loose."

"Murderer?" Brittany sets the bag on the counter. "Who died?"

Dylan says, "Zach. At Renee's shop. And the reason Raphe

isn't returning your texts is because he surrendered his electronics to us."

"That's horrible. Who'd want to kill Zach?" Brittany picks up a cookie and hands it to Dylan. "You don't think Raphe had anything to do with it, do you?"

"Don't know yet. Do you?" Dylan glances my way as he inhales the cookie in two bites.

That's my cue to tell Brittany what I planned to say about Raphe. "Dylan thinks it's probably best to keep your distance from Raphe until we sort things out."

"Dylan, huh?" Brittany crosses her arms. "Are you going to keep your distance from Renee, then, too? It's her shop."

The kid makes an annoyingly good point. "We need to find Renee first."

"You still haven't found her?" Brittany's face quickly morphs from belligerent to concerned.

I shake my head as I pop the pizza into the oven. "We think she went on a bike ride. It's getting dark, so I'm sure she'll be back soon." I hope with all my heart.

Dylan leans against the center island. "When was the last time you saw Zach, Brittany?"

"It was about four thirty, I think. He asked if he could use a computer to print something out. He said his phone went missing, and he needed a code."

As I fill two glasses with water, I ask, "A code for what?"

"I didn't ask." Brittany shrugs. "I was too busy running errands for Angelica."

"Which computer did he use?" Dylan asks as he swipes another cookie.

"The laptop. I told him where the printer is in the storeroom, and then I guess he left out the back."

I'm still pondering what kind of code Zach needed when it hits me. "The code for the back door of Renee's shop?" I turn to Dylan for confirmation.

"No comment. But I'm going to need that laptop. And access to your security camera files." Dylan turns his attention back to Brittany. "Did Zach have a phone when he arrived?"

"Yeah." Brittany pulls out a stool at the island and sits. "I saw him texting."

"Me too." I set the plates and glasses of water on the table in the nook. I've been holding something back from Dylan, but maybe it's time to spill. "Renee told me something in confidence, but you're going to find out anyway if you look at Zach's texts and emails. I hope it's why Renee left her phone in the shop."

Dylan's third cookie stops halfway to his mouth. "What?"

"Zach has been texting and emailing Renee nonstop ever since we found out he and Angelica were coming to town. He's been suggesting they, um…" Man, Renee is going to kill me.

"They what?" Brittany's eyes are as big as saucers.

I hate that I'm betraying Renee, but it's better Dylan knows now. Before he finds the messages on his own. It'll look suspicious. "I guess Zach and Angelica haven't been getting along for months. He suggested he and Renee should talk. About getting back together."

"Shut. Up." Brittany's mouth drops. "Not after what he did to her. She told him to take a hike, right?"

"Not exactly." This is where things get sticky. "She agreed to meet him in the city. For coffee and some closure. Nothing more. But he never showed. Gave her some excuse about not being able to get away without Angelica finding out. She's his meal ticket, so he can't afford to upset her."

"When was this?" Dylan asks.

"Last week. But after Zach didn't show, Renee stopped returning his messages. She said she was through with him for good." Maybe I shouldn't have said the "for good" part.

Dylan pinches the bridge of his nose like he has a headache. "I better get your computer and security files tonight. Can I take the pizza to go?"

"Sure." I grab the barely warm pizza from the oven and put four pieces onto a paper plate. "Let's go."

Brittany says, "I want to go too. Give me two minutes."

Before I can protest, she's out of the kitchen and banging up the stairs.

I hand a piece of pizza to Dylan. "You wanted to ask me questions about Zach over dinner. What were they?"

"I didn't say the questions were about the case. You said you wanted to talk later, and while I eat is the only time I have. And because I'm really tired of eating alone." He stuffs pizza into his mouth so he doesn't have to finish the thought.

An old technique that's equally annoying today as it was years ago.

"So just anyone would do to keep you company?"

After he swallows, he says, "You're always my first choice." Dylan hitches his brows as he stuffs another big bite into his mouth in his hurry to eat.

He'd thrown down the gauntlet about dating Gage this morning. Dylan knows that when he pushes me in one direction, I usually go the other just for form. At least until I can process and make the idea my own.

Well, his little reverse psychology technique isn't going to work this time.

Leaning close, I whisper, "I'm on to you and your sneaky —" Brittany is clomping down the stairs, so I stop.

He whispers back, "Thanks for having dinner with me anyway. Sort of." Dylan's phone rings as he's stuffing more pizza into his mouth. He answers, "Mmmm?"

Brittany joins us, and we both wait while Dylan nods as he listens. Finally, he says, "I'll be right there." After he hangs up, he says, "We found Renee. She had a flat and was walking her bike back to town."

Thank goodness. "That's weird about her flat. She's a seasoned rider. She always has a patch kit."

"Hmmm. Gotta go." Dylan grabs another piece of pizza. "Can you send me a link and passwords to access your security files online? I'll pick up the laptop in the morning. Don't touch it."

I have to squelch the urge to roll my eyes. I'm trying to set a good example for Brittany. "Obviously." I grab the leftover quiche in my fridge for Renee. She must be starving. "But we're coming too."

"Yeah." Brittany nods in agreement.

"Negative. Renee is at the clinic. She has scratches and bruises that need to be treated and photographed."

My stomach drops. "Like she-fell-off-her-bike wounds? Or like she-got-into-a-fight-with-a-man injuries?"

Dylan's jaw clenches. "They can look alike."

CHAPTER 5

The ceiling in my mom's old bedroom has thirty-two small cracks and three big ones I should probably be worried about. A fact I didn't know until tonight. The moon is overly bright, making the cracks stand out, and I can't sleep for worrying over Renee.

My phone buzzes on my nightstand at almost eleven thirty, startling me. As I lunge for it, I'm hoping it's Renee. Or Dylan. But it's Gage, my lawyer. I whisper so I don't wake Brittany. "Hi. What's up?"

"Sorry to call so late, but Renee wants to come over. Dylan took her phone, so she asked me to call. She said you wouldn't mind."

"Of course not. I'm up anyway."

"Good. We'll be there in a few. We need to discuss something with you."

"'Kay." After I disconnect the call, I throw the covers back and hop into my robe and slippers. Normally, I'd care what my hair and naked face look like in front of tall, handsome Gage. He's blond with green eyes and wears glasses that make him look even smarter than he is, but my only concern right now is for Renee. That Gage is bringing her must mean she called him for help even though Gage isn't a criminal lawyer. He mostly does trusts and family law. However, he's the only lawyer in town.

It's hard to think of Renee needing a criminal lawyer, but there are way too many incriminating details stacking up against her. I'm glad she got some legal help.

Navigating the hall, trying to miss the spots that have moaned with age ever since I was a kid, I continue to do my best not to wake Brittany. Cooper is creeping slowly behind me as if scared something is going to jump out at him. I don't call him Chicken Coop for nothing.

When we finally make it to the kitchen, I flip on the lights and override my coffeepot. I have it timed to make my coffee automatically each morning because heaven forbid I have to wait an extra fifteen minutes for my caffeine fix. The machine is just starting to rumble when there's a quiet knock at my back door.

Cooper runs for the door, wagging his tail. He's no watchdog. He's more into making friends with anyone he meets.

Pushing the door's curtain aside, I confirm it's Renee and Gage before I open it. Renee looks like she got into a bar fight. She has a bruise on her cheek and scratches on her face and neck. I don't even bother to say hello. I just wrap her up in a hug.

With a grunt, Renee hugs me back. "Gently, please. I hurt all over."

"Oh. Sorry." I quickly release her. Then I smile at Gage. "Hi. Come in. Anyone want coffee?"

Renee says, "I'd rather have a glass of wine," as she leans down to say hello to Cooper. "And maybe a doggy hug too." Cooper happily complies.

"Wine it is." I grab a bottle from the rack. When I turn around to get the opener, Gage is behind me with it in his hand.

"I remembered where you kept it from the last time you cooked me an incredible dinner. May I?"

"Please." I hand him the bottle and then reach into the cabinet to grab three glasses.

"You want me to stay, Renee? Or leave you two to talk?" Gage asks as he pushes up his glasses with his index finger.

Renee smiles weakly. "It's late. If you'd rather go home and get some rest, that's fine. Either way, thanks for coming to my rescue tonight."

Gage nods. "No worries." Then he turns to me. "You must have a million questions."

Boy, do I ever. But Renee looks like she's been through a lot, so I turn her way. "First, are you okay? Can I get you anything else?"

"I'm just sore." Renee takes a deep drink from her glass.

"And stuck here in town until further notice. Dylan is acting like he doesn't believe I had nothing to do with Zach's death."

"It's his job to make you think he doesn't believe you," Gage says as he pulls out two stools from under the center island and holds out a hand. "Have a seat, both of you, and let's chat about Dylan."

Curious, I slip beside Renee. "What about him?"

Renee glares at Gage, before she says to me, "Gage thinks it's better I don't discuss the case with you. Because you might accidentally say something incriminating to Dylan. Since you and he..." Renee shakes her head and takes another long sip from her glass. "Whatever you and he are doing right now."

Gage's brows rise as he waits for a definition of my relationship with Dylan too.

I sip my wine as I think about my answer. "Dylan's my brother-in-law. Anything beyond that hasn't been explored or decided. Mostly because Dylan wants me to date you, Gage."

"I think that's a great idea." A big grin lights up Gage's face.

His enthusiasm warms me inside, but at the same time, he needs to know Dylan's motives. "Dylan wants me to date you because he believes if I do, I'll figure out I'm still in love with him. And full disclosure, we kissed this morning. He wanted to prove his point."

Gage's smile quickly dims. "That kiss proves *my* point. You and Renee shouldn't discuss this case."

"That's like setting a jar of cookies in front of a hungry two-year-old and telling her not to eat one." I take Renee's hand. "We tell each other everything. Don't we?" Is there something Renee hasn't told me about Zach?

"Yes." She turns to Gage. "What if Sawyer promises to refrain from discussing me at all with Dylan. Will that do?"

Gage says, "Do you think you can do that, Sawyer? You and Madge earned yourselves a reputation for sticking your noses where they didn't belong when Chad died at your shop. It almost got you killed."

My stomach takes a dive at the memory. I could've been killed if Dylan hadn't saved me. "It was my stuff they were trying to steal. I was involved whether I liked it or not. I wasn't just going to sit around and do nothing."

"Again, proving my point." Gage takes a long drink from his glass. "You speak to Dylan almost every day."

True. Because he makes sure that happens. "I talk to a lot of people every day."

Gage nods. "You might learn something that could put you in a difficult position."

Renee and Dylan are two of the three people I trust most in the world. Along with my sister, Meg. Well, in Dylan's case, I don't trust him with my heart again...yet. But I believe in him in every other way. He's genuinely a kind, decent guy.

Still, what if Renee does tell me something that Dylan needs to know? Or vice versa. It *could* leave me in a tight spot. But in my heart, I know Renee is innocent and that Dylan will figure out how to prove it. "I can handle it."

Renee pours herself more wine. "She's guarded every secret I've ever trusted her with."

"Fine." Gage sets down his glass. "I'm going to bed. Good night." He heads toward the back door.

"Wait." I catch up and lay a hand on his sleeve. "I didn't mean to upset you by telling you about that kiss. I just want to be completely honest." Gage told me once that he'd had a crush on me since we were both teenagers. I want to tread lightly with his heart.

"I'm always up for a fair competition. So, when things calm down a bit, I'd like the chance to kiss you too. Before you make up your mind. Night, Sawyer." He opens the door and heads out into the dark.

"Night." I lock up and let out a long sigh. Gage has a point. It's always better to compare apples to apples. Or in this case, kisses to kisses.

AFTER RENEE BORROWS some sweats to change into and Cooper has gone to sleep on his doggy bed in my room, Renee and I settle into the well-worn antique furniture in the living room. The deep indents from former occupants sink us into the cozy couch, but at the same time, there's probably a serious risk that we might fall through to the frame any second. I should replace the old furniture, but my mom loved the original red upholstery, so I don't have the heart just yet.

After I take a sip of wine, I ask, "What happened today? Start from after you brought us ice cream."

Renee sighs as she tucks her bare feet underneath her. "I went back to the shop and cleaned up a bit before Annie arrived for first shift. I helped her with the lunch crowd and then told her I was going for a bike ride. Raphe was due in to help her with the early afternoon shift, and then Z was going to come later. I went home, changed, and took off for a new trail I hadn't ridden before. While I was riding, I didn't see a root sticking up and fell off my bike, sliding head over heels down a steep slope. It bent my front wheel badly enough, I couldn't fix the flat, so I started walking home. Next thing I know, I'm a suspect for Zach's murder."

Renee sips her wine as tears form. "I hated what Zach did to me, but I'd never wish something as horrible as this on him."

"Of course you wouldn't. But what about the email he had with him? Did Dylan show you that? Was it a code for your back door?"

"Yes, but I didn't send it. I was trying to avoid Zach. Not give him Annie's code for access."

This makes me sit up. "Annie's code?"

Renee nods. "I give all my employees different codes. They use the back door when they come on and off shift because it's next to the electronic time clock. All their hours are tallied so the system can create their paychecks. If they forget to clock out, the door records tell me when they left.

All the employees know to only use their own codes because of it."

"Someone must've hacked your computer to get the codes. Possibly Annie's home computer as well?" Skills way above my knowledge level.

"Yeah. It looks that way. But I'm not even sure Annie does more than read email on her computer, so it's probably just my electronics that got hacked."

Annie used to tell us back in high school English class that reading a book was the only acceptable way to pass the time. She claimed to have never owned a television. I add, "Z said Annie went home early because she wasn't feeling well. But she stopped by the bookshop first to get an autograph."

Renee nods. "That doesn't surprise me. Annie takes credit for discovering and encouraging Angelica. She'll tell anyone who'll listen. I think she still beta reads for Angelica." Renee shakes her head. "I'm kicking myself for only installing cameras in the retail area. But nobody is going to steal ice cream. It'd be money from the till if I got robbed. If I'd had cameras in the back too, it would have proved my innocence. Now it's only my word against a bunch of evidence."

"Speaking of that, you didn't notice the empty outline for the sledgehammer above the workbench when you grabbed your bike?"

"I haven't gone into the shed in weeks. I've been leaving my bike on the side of the deck because the weather has been so nice."

So that hammer could've been stolen and returned

without her knowledge. "Who knows where your house key is? Besides me."

She shrugs. "Our neighbors used it to water plants while we were away when I was a kid. Z and Annie water my plants now when I'm gone. I'll have to call my parents and ask."

"Did Zach know where you hid the key?"

"Yes." Renee frowns into her wineglass. "He used to lift the pot for me when I forgot to bring my keys to school."

Which was always, because she knew the spare would be in its proper hiding place. Her controlling father made sure of that. "I hate to ask, but is there any chance that Zach was just in the wrong place at the wrong time? Could that hammer have been meant for you?"

"Dylan and I discussed that." Renee stands to pace but ends up limping more than pacing. "He asked if I had any reason to believe I'm in danger or know of anyone who'd want to hurt me but come on…it's me here. I never sent that email Zach had in his hand. Someone is trying to make it look like I lured him to my store and killed him. But who?"

That's the question of the moment. "Did Zach mention he was in any sort of trouble when you spoke to him last week?"

"I never actually spoke to him. It was all online. You know I told him I never wanted to speak to him again when we broke up. I thought he was respecting my wishes." Renee huffs out a breath. "I wonder if I was even communicating with Zach? What if whoever hacked my account was who I was really conversing with?"

That's an interesting thought. "If that's true, it'd make sense of why Zach never showed up for your meeting in the city last week after begging you to come."

"Yeah. It would." Renee sits on the other end of the couch again and faces me. "Maybe whoever set that meeting up wanted me out of my house and shop for a few hours. So they could get what they needed to set me up."

I nod as I do the math. "It takes at least forty-five minutes to get to downtown San Francisco from here if the traffic is light. And of course, you'd wait for a few minutes for Zach to arrive before you drove all the way back. Wait a minute." My mind races back to the short conversation I had with Zach earlier. "Zach asked me today if you were still around. I thought he meant were you still at the shop, working, but maybe he was asking if you were still living in town. Because he didn't know if you'd moved away or not. You and he haven't had any contact since he left, have you?"

She slowly shakes her head. "No. Not until a few weeks ago when I started getting all the emails and texts. Apologizing, and asking me to rekindle our relationship."

A shiver runs up my spine at the thought of someone sneaking around Renee's house and electronics. "You're welcome to stay here until we get to the bottom of things. In the meantime, let's change the locks at your house and the store. We should also find someone to look at all your electronics. To be sure they're secure."

"Agreed. And I'll take you up on staying here. I'd be too freaked out to sleep at my house tonight."

"Great." I plaster on a reassuring smile. "We'll figure this out. I promise."

"Let's hope." Renee sets her empty glass down and gives me a hug. "Thank you, Sawyer. For not asking if I killed Zach. You know I didn't. I'm so glad you moved back home. I've never had a better friend."

"Me neither." A big lump grows in my throat. "Let's get you settled in Meg's old room. We'll worry about things in the morning." We start toward the stairs.

Renee wipes away her tears. "Are you sure about Dylan, though? I could keep my distance from you until this is over. Stay in the B&B. I don't want to mess up whatever is going on with you guys by putting you in the middle."

"I can handle Dylan. Don't worry about that."

"He's never talked to me like he did at the station. He thinks I did it, Sawyer. Gage even told me not to answer a few of Dylan's questions tonight. He might pressure you to spill about what I've told you. To see if it lines up. It's his job."

That *could* cause a huge rift between Dylan and me. Mostly because he has to know a job can't come first with me before my best friend. I'd better talk to him first thing tomorrow. Set some boundaries. "If Dylan really thought you were guilty, he would've arrested you." I rub a hand up and down her back while I lead her up the stairs. "Let's just get some sleep now. Okay?"

"Yep. I'm beat," Renee says as she slowly limps up the stairs beside me.

After I get Renee settled in my sister's former bedroom, I

head for the master. Brittany is stretched out on my bed, leaning back against the headboard, waiting for me.

I whisper, "It's late. Why aren't you in your own bed?"

Brittany crosses her arms. "So, I have to stay away from Raphe, while you invite the chief murder suspect to stay with us? In what universe is this fair?"

I'm too tired to deal with this. "It's not fair. But I know Renee didn't do anything wrong. I've known her my whole life. Can you say the same for Raphe?" I know she can't because Raphe's family moved to town recently.

"No. But he didn't even know Zach."

Cooper lets out a loud sigh and curls up in a ball, not interested in this argument either. "Better safe than sorry. Let's fight in the morning." I toss my thumb over my shoulder. "Go to bed or move over. I'm exhausted."

Brittany is chewing her bottom lip. Something she does when she's thinking. Or scheming. Finally, she says, "Full disclosure. I was sitting at the foot of the stairs and heard everything you guys said. So, I should maybe tell you something. But it doesn't have anything to do with Zach's death. It's about Raphe."

Uh-oh. "What?"

Brittany grimaces. "He's been on restriction for the last month. For hacking into online gamers' accounts and stealing things the other players have won. His dad caught him red-handed. Because his dad wrote the game."

"Did his parents tell Dylan this earlier?"

Brittany shakes her head. "His parents said it was a family

matter. No one else's business because no one got hurt. His dad put all the stolen things back into people's accounts."

I sink to the side of the bed. "How do *you* know this if the police took Raphe's electronics?"

"If you were even remotely up on gaming, you'd know that you can chat with other players through the game. I play it too."

"Do you steal from other players too?" I don't care if it's just a game. Stealing is stealing in my book.

"No. Stealing game pieces is something the really smart computer nerds do. I can't be bothered. But it doesn't have anything to do with Zach."

"If that's true, then why tell me?"

Brittany's gaze drops to her chewed-up fingernails. "Because you took me in and gave me a nice home. I didn't want you to kick me out if you found out later and thought I lied to you."

My outrage at the stealing is replaced by sympathy for a kid whose mother abandoned her. I was lucky to have a mother with a huge heart. I can see why she found room in it to include Brittany. "I wouldn't kick you out. But I'd probably make you wax every wood surface in this monstrosity."

Her lips tilt slightly. "'Kay. But you can't tell Dylan. It'll look bad for Raphe. And he'll know I told you. You have to promise." Brittany rolls out of bed and heads for the door. "Good night."

"Night."

Promise not to tell Dylan about a hacker?

And here I was worried about keeping Renee's confidence. Now I have to add Brittany's too? I'm not sure I can do that.

It's only been hours since Zach died, and I'm already finding myself between the hammer and the anvil.

CHAPTER 6

*U*nable to sleep past 6:00 a.m., I'm sipping coffee in the kitchen early Sunday morning. And looking at the surveillance recordings from yesterday's book signing. Zach has his cell phone in his hand when he comes in the shop, and Angelica is talking on hers. I'm hoping I can see how Zach misplaced his phone at the bookshop so we can find it. There must be a ton of information on it.

It's surreal to watch Zach smile and flirt with all the ladies, unaware that within a few hours, he'll be dead. It sends a shiver up my spine just as a quiet knock sounds on my back door.

Happy for the interruption, I pause the video to see who's here so early. I push the curtain aside to check and open the door to a rumpled-looking sheriff with sexy five-o'clock shadow.

I croak out, "Morning. Coffee?" Usually, I'm incapable of having lucid conversations before my second cup of joe. I might have to buck it up this morning. Or slam down another cup.

"Coffee sounds good." Dylan quietly closes the door behind him. "Are Renee and Brittany still sleeping?"

News travels fast in small towns. "How could you possibly know Renee spent the night?"

"It's my job to know where Renee is until we get to the bottom of things." Dylan's head swivels around as he searches for something. "Any cookies left? I'm starving."

"Anyone who is mean to my best friend doesn't deserve cookies."

"I wasn't mean. Just doing my job." Dylan pulls out a stool next to the one I was sitting on at the center island and flops onto it. "Where's Cooper?"

"In Brittany's room, sleeping like I should be. Don't try to change the subject."

He lifts his hands. "What was the subject again?"

"Renee. We both know she didn't kill anyone. So, quit treating her like a criminal." I pour Dylan a mug and top off mine. "And until you find the person who actually killed Zach, you and I aren't going to talk about Renee. At all. Got it?" I hadn't meant to be so short with Dylan. Luckily, he knows I'm not good company before coffee.

"Fine with me." He points to my laptop's screen. "I see you're back at it. Did you figure out what happened to Zach's phone?"

"Not yet. Watching the video is sort of creeping me out."

"Since it's your recording, I'll save you some sleuthing." He takes a long drink. "Angelica's phone died, so she borrowed Zach's to make a call in the back while on one of her bathroom breaks. When she's done, she drops the phone in her purse and hurries back to the line of waiting customers. Later, when Zach asks for his phone back, Angelica looks around but says she doesn't remember where she put it before she goes back to chatting with an excited fan."

So, nothing nefarious happened to his phone. "Did you get the phone back from Angelica, then?"

He nods. "I need to get the laptop from your store too. If you'd like, I can borrow a key and get it myself. I won't bother you anymore after that."

Bother me? Now I feel like a total jerk. "I'm sorry for snapping at you, Dylan. I'm just really worried about Renee."

"Understood. And I shouldn't have stopped by so early. I forgot what a grump you are without caffeine flowing freely through your veins."

"Will you forgive me if I make you breakfast?"

"Always." Dylan drains his mug. "I'll get the computer and be right back."

"'Kay." I grab the keys from my purse and hand them over. "The alarm code is my birthday."

Dylan accepts the keys with a frown. "That's not a secure pass—"

"I know." Using both hands, I push Dylan toward the

door. "If you promise not to lecture me again about my bad passwords, I'll make your favorite eggs."

Dylan glances over his shoulder and grins. "Benedict?"

"Yes. With extra hollandaise. Now go before I change my mind."

He turns and leans his mouth near my ear. The stubble on his chin tickles as he whispers, "I haven't had eggs Benedict since the last time you made them for me."

"Really? In eight years?" I lean back and blink at him. "Why not?"

"Because they're your favorite too. It didn't seem right to eat them without you." He gives me a quick kiss before he turns to leave.

I open my mouth to reply, but by the time my brain reengages, he's already halfway out the door. My lips and cheek still tingle from his touch when I turn around to meet two unhappy women. Both Brittany and Renee are standing with their arms crossed and their brows arched.

How much of that did they hear?

I force a smile. "Morning, guys. Who wants eggs Bene?" Cooper bounds out from behind Brittany's legs and runs toward me for his morning dose of love.

Brittany says, "Way to keep your distance from Dylan. Did you rat me out about Raphe?"

"No." After giving Cooper a rub all over, I let him out the back door to do his business. "I didn't say a word about that. And I didn't say I wasn't going to speak to Dylan. I said I wouldn't discuss Renee with him."

Renee nods. "That's true. But the last thing I thought I'd see was you kissing Dylan before breakfast." She turns to Brittany, "What about Raphe?"

I'll let them talk amongst themselves while I get the water ready to poach the eggs. And try not to be incredibly touched that Dylan wouldn't eat eggs Benedict without me in all these years.

THE HOLLANDAISE IS ALMOST DONE when another knock sounds on my back door. Assuming it's Dylan, and afraid to stop stirring the delicate sauce, I call out, "It's open. Come in."

Gage sticks his blond head inside the door. "Morning. Am I interrupting?" He leans down to pet Cooper, who's lifting a paw for a high five.

"Nope. Come in and have some breakfast," I say without thinking through the logistics of sharing breakfast with Dylan and Gage while not discussing Renee or what happened yesterday.

On top of that, Renee and Brittany had decided we'd keep Raphe's online stealing activity to ourselves for now. I'm not in agreement with that. I think Brittany should tell Dylan herself. But one problem at a time this morning. "Everyone sit. Let's eat while it's hot." I can't imagine what's taking Dylan so long, but I don't want to let everyone's eggs get cold.

Gage, Renee, and Brittany all gather in the nook, chatting quietly about something. Hopefully, they're telling him about Raphe.

I set plates on the table with English muffins topped with Canadian bacon, poached eggs, and avocado slices all swimming in rich hollandaise.

Gage looks up and grins. "Thank you. These are my favorite."

"Welcome." Of course, they'd be Gage's favorite too. Guilt for thinking of eating them without Dylan sets in heavy, so I pick up my cell and text Dylan to ask where he is.

Just as I grab my plate to join the others, my phone dings with a reply. "Dylan had to go back to the office. I should run a plate over to him. You guys go ahead and eat."

Three curious sets of eyes turn my way, so I say, "What? I promise I won't talk about Renee."

Gage sets down his fork. "I'd be happy to run the eggs over to his office. Please. Sit and enjoy your breakfast."

Okay, that backfired. My mind scrambles for another excuse to eat with Dylan. "Actually, I'm hoping Dylan called Madge in today so we can get the latest scoop on the case. She's a font of information. The egg delivery will help me get caught up with all the things Dylan won't tell me." But I'll eat with Dylan first. Then get the scoop if Madge is there.

Renee's gaze meets mine. She knows me too well. And she probably heard what Dylan said to me about not eating eggs Benedict without me.

"Then, by all means, go," Renee says with a smirk. "You

and Madge make a killer investigating team. Just get back here and report as soon as you can, please."

Grateful for the backup, I nod and pack up breakfast. "Be back in a flash."

The trek is all downhill from my house, keeping my pace quick. After I cross the busy grassy town square across from my store, I tug on the glass doors to the municipal building and head for the police station. Inside, among the clatter of deputies tapping their keyboards, Madge is at her desk, talking on the phone. She glances at the food containers in my hands and then points toward Dylan's office, giving me the go-ahead to join him.

Rapping the doorframe with my knuckle forces Dylan's gaze from his computer screen toward me.

He smiles as he sneaks a candy bar wrapper into the trash. "Hey. Sorry, I had to skip out on breakfast."

I lift the containers. "Brought it with me. And I'll join you." I sit and start to remove all the tops.

"Wait." He holds up a hand. "While it's appreciated, I don't have time. Angelica will be here any second."

"Oh. Okay." As I pack up, I add, "You probably need to ask Angelica about her former assistant, Kate, right? Maybe see if she has any computer skills? Enough to be able to hack into Renee's computers?"

"None of your business, Ms. Don't Discuss Renee With Me." Dylan's eyes twinkle with amusement. "And I'm not falling for food bribes." He hands over my keys and digs a piece of paper out from a pile on his desk. "Here's the receipt for your laptop. I'll get it back as soon as I can. Now if you'll excuse me, please?"

A little offended that he thought I brought him food only for information—I planned to get that from Madge, not him—I accept the paper and then slip his half of the breakfast toward him anyway. "You eat so fast you'll have plenty of time to have something more than a candy bar before she gets here. I'll get out of your hair now." I turn and walk toward the door.

"Sawyer?"

I stop and turn around. "What?"

"Wait a sec." He pops the top off his breakfast and takes a bite. After he swallows, he says, "Amazing. As always. Thank you." Then he grins at me.

I'm such a sucker for that smile. "Welcome. Talk to you later?"

He nods as he stuffs another bite into his mouth.

Armed with my eggs, I head for Madge's desk. Just when I'm about to flop in her guest chair, the station's front door opens. Angelica, wearing dark glasses and with her hair a rat's nest, enters the station and then stops as the door swings shut behind her. Wearing designer athleisurewear and sparkly tennis shoes, she tugs off her sunglasses to reveal bloodshot eyes and ruined mascara. She sees me and says, "Hi, Sawyer. Do you know where Dylan's office is?"

"That one right there. In the corner." I point the way. "I'm so sorry about Zach, Angelica."

"Thank you," she whispers as she hitches her huge purse

higher on her shoulder and walks toward Dylan's office with the speed of a prisoner approaching a firing squad. It must be awful to be questioned the day after her husband has been brutally murdered.

With sympathy filling my heart, I sit in front of Madge's desk and open my breakfast. "Want some?" I tilt the container her way.

Shaking her head, Madge says, "I had a big breakfast earlier."

"'Kay." I take a bite of my breakfast and moan. The yolky, eggy goodness all soaked into the nooks and crannies of the English muffin is fantastic.

"That must be a heck of a lot better than my boring pancakes were," Madge says with a smile. "How's it going with Brittany? Dylan told me she's upset with you for ruining her date with Raphe."

"Yep." I want to tell Madge about Raphe's game hacking, but I don't want to upset Brittany. "How old were your girls when you let them start dating?"

"If it'd been up to Norm, our kids would have had to wait until they turned thirty. We compromised on sixteen. But if they didn't answer our texts right away, they lost all dating privileges."

That seems reasonable to me. "Do you think if I tell Brittany she can't date Raphe until next year, she'd hate me forever?"

"Being hated," Madge makes air quotes with her fingers,

"often comes with raising kids. But now that my girls are in college, we're all best pals."

"That's nice to hear. It's just that I've only been Brittany's guardian a few weeks and she's not used to having many rules."

Madge reaches out and squeezes my hand. "All kids are different. Some are ready to date earlier than others. Just go with your gut."

"The only gut I have is from eating too many cookies, not from years of parenting experience."

Madge chuckles. "It's obvious how much Brittany adores you. She's happy again since you've been back. It'll all work out."

"Thanks, Madge." That made my new guardian's heart go gooey. "And you're right. I need to man up. I'll have another talk with Brittany. Be tough. Lay down the rules."

"Atta girl." Madge leans back in her squeaky chair. "Have you heard the latest in Zach's case?"

"Nope." This is why I love Madge. I don't even have to ask for the lowdown. She just tells me.

"Well," Madge leans closer, "Ben told me that he contacted Angelica's former assistant and broke the news about Zach's death. He said she was distraught but more than happy to spill her guts about working for Angelica. She hated her demanding boss with a passion. But the even bigger news is, Zach and the assistant, what's her name, had an affair."

"Kate," I add as I take another bite. This doesn't surprise

me. Zach cheated on Renee too. Once a cheater... "When was the affair?"

"As far as Kate knew, they were still having it. She said she quit working for Angelica a few weeks ago because Zach promised to leave his wife soon. Then Kate and Zach were going to be together."

"Angelica made it sound like she fired Kate." Could Kate have found out about the texts and emails Zach sent Renee? Maybe she was mad enough to take revenge on Renee? I need to find out what exactly was in those emails.

"One of them is lying," Madge says. "And get this. Kate has a business degree with a minor in computer science."

Giving her the potential skills to hack Renee's computers. "Did Angelica know about the affair?"

Madge shrugs. "Not sure she'd care. Kate said Angelica was so busy working with her ghostwriter, she'd probably never notice. Seems Angelica lost her muse or something and hasn't written anything on her own for years now. Kate was the one who found the ghostwriter for Angelica in the first place, single-handedly saving Angelica's career."

More like the ghostwriter did. Looks like the Admiral was right in his theory about Angelica not writing her own books. "When I googled Kate before going to bed last night, the pictures made it look like she traveled with Angelica and Zach to all her events. But Kate was always in the background. One photo caption said she was the husband and wife's assistant. If Kate was Zach's assistant too, she might have had access to his passwords."

The station phones rings, and Madge holds up a finger before answering. After she hangs up, she says, "Yeah, but here's the rub. Kate says she's been away visiting family since she quit her job. She's still in Florida. No way she could have killed Zach."

Huh. That's an interesting twist. "She could've hired someone to do it."

"I don't know. But it gets even worse for Renee."

My stomach clenches, so I push my breakfast aside. "How so?"

Madge looks around to be sure no one is listening before she says, "Mr. Martinez says he thought he saw Renee go in the back door to her shop around four o'clock yesterday."

Mr. Martinez owns the gallery next door to Renee's shop. He's older and wears thick glasses because he's practically blind. "That's impossible. Renee was riding her bike then."

Madge leans even closer. "You guys need to find Renee a witness from the bike paths, or maybe think about hiring a lawyer from the city. Without a witness, Dylan might have to arrest her."

Arrest Renee?

I have to stop that from happening. She needs a break, and I'm going to find one for her. But where to start?

CHAPTER 7

*A*fter a quick stop at home to grab some plates of Brittany's cookies, I head for Mr. Martinez's shop. He keeps his art gallery open for the tourists every day, never takes a day off. He's a lonely widower, and he likes to chat with his customers.

A bell tinkles overhead as I enter the musty art gallery. Large paintings of waves crashing against the Pacific shoreline hang on the walls. Sculptures of seagulls, pelicans, and other friendly sea creatures are scattered about the showroom, all designed to encourage the tourists to bring a piece of coastal life back to their homes. The first year I moved away, Mr. Martinez sent me a painting to hang on my apartment wall in Chicago so I wouldn't forget where I grew up. That's what a kind man he is.

Mr. Martinez sits behind the counter in the back with his chin resting on his chest, snoring so loud, it's a wonder he doesn't wake himself, much less the dead.

"Mr. Martinez?" I call out, but to no avail. "Hello?"

Not sure what to do next, short of poking him awake, I head to the rear and stop in front of the desk. There's a bell on the counter, so I smack it as hard as I can.

Mr. Martinez's head jerks up, and he bats his eyes like he's trying to remember where he is. Finally, his gaze focuses on mine, and he says, "Hi, Sawyer. Need some art?"

"Not today, thanks. Want some cookies?" I slide a paper plate under his nose. "Brittany is becoming an amazing baker. And I know you love a good sugar cookie." I've been baking things for Mr. Martinez since I came back to live in Sunset Cove. He's so thin, I worry he doesn't eat enough.

"Yes, please." His frail fingers grab a frosted treat, and he takes a huge bite. Nodding, he declares, "You've taught her well, Sawyer. This is a darn good cookie. I think I'll have another."

"I'll let Brittany know you liked them, but first, can I ask you a question? About Renee. Are you sure it was her you saw around four yesterday afternoon?" I don't want to sound like I doubt his story, but I do.

Mr. Martinez nods between bites. "I set that alarm clock to go off at four o'clock each day so I don't forget to take my pills." He points to an old-fashioned wind-up clock on the counter. "I had just taken my meds before I went out back to empty the trash. That's when I saw her. She punched in her code and went in through the back door like she always does."

He only saw the back of a person? That's encouraging. "What was she wearing?"

"Dark clothes." A frown creases his forehead. "Jeans, I think, and a black sweatshirt. Tennis shoes. Had her hair stuffed under a ball cap."

Odd. Renee is always dressed like she's got a hot date later. Which she generally does. "Anything else? Did she have a purse or a bag with her?" The murderer had to carry the sledgehammer in something. No one would just walk around with something obvious like that.

He pushes up his bottle-thick glasses. "A big black bag, I think. I know it was her, though, because of that fancy watch she wears. You know, the one that can do almost anything except mop the floors? Saw it when she lifted her hand to punch in the code."

Renee does have a tech-savvy watch. But so do a lot of people. "Wait. Are you saying she punched in the code with the same hand the watch was on?"

"Yes. Why?"

"Because Renee is left-handed and wears the watch on her right wrist. Wouldn't most people use their dominant hand to punch in a code?"

"Maybe it was the left she used. I wasn't paying all that much attention." He shrugs. "All I know is that I called out to her because I wanted to talk to her about the next merchant meeting. Then I saw the cords hanging down from her ears and figured she couldn't hear me because she was listening to music."

Renee has new wireless earbuds that play music from her watch. She'd just shown them to me the other day when she was explaining why I needed a smartwatch too. But I don't need a device yelling at me to stand up or exercise more. My guilty conscience is already good at that. However, she has regular earphones too. "Okay. Well, thanks. I'll tell Brittany how much you liked her cookies. Have a good day."

"You too, Sawyer. Wait." He lifts a bony finger. "Will I see you next week at the merchants' meeting? We're going to vote on those compliance issues, you know."

Great. My bookshop is one of the stores on the square whose front isn't like everyone else's. My mom was the free-spirited type who thought complying to anything was a cop-out. Individualism was her mantra. "I'll try to make it."

But I won't try very hard. I have bigger worries right now. Like helping Renee stay out of jail.

I push the door open and head outside.

Armed with another plate of cookies, I take a big gulp of salty ocean-scented air to replace the stale aroma of the art gallery and walk up the hill toward Annie's house. She lives with her husband Charlie in a cool Craftsman-style bungalow that I used to pass each morning on my way to school. Her husband was the town's carpenter until he finally retired a few years ago, so their home, unlike mine, always looks impeccable. Like right out of an architectural digest or something.

Since Wade, the carpenter my mom had hired to fix all the rotting wood in my Victorian, is now in jail for killing his best friend, I've been planning to ask Charlie if he'd consider working on my house. And I really want to talk to Annie about how someone could get her door code to the ice-cream shop. Hopefully, I can casually slip some questions in while she's in a cookie coma.

I lift my hand to knock on the front door, but before I can make contact, it swings open. Charlie, a graying, short, stout man, with a ruddy complexion, smiles at me.

"Heya, Sawyer. Saw you coming up the walk. What brings you by?"

I thrust the cookies his way. "Thought I'd try to bribe you out of retirement. My old house really needs someone as skilled as you to bring her back to the way she was in her glory days."

"It *is* hard to find skilled craftspeople anymore." Charlie lifts the plastic wrap and picks up a cookie. "Do baked goods come as part of the deal?"

"Absolutely. I had a similar deal with Wade. His estimate to do the job included full access to all the leftovers in my fridge plus a little over thirty thousand dollars. But I can only pay you as much as four thousand nine hundred and ninety-nine dollars at a time."

Charlie's bushy brows arch. "Why's that?"

I hate to air family business for all to see, but it's a weird legal requirement I have to live with. "My grandparents set my mom's trust up so that my uncle has to approve any spending over five grand. I'd rather not have to beg him for money. Or justify the repairs."

Charlie slowly nods as he swallows. "Understood. No one dislikes dealing with your uncle more than me. He was the bane of my existence when I did work for the city."

"Well then, are you interested?"

Before he can answer, Annie appears from the kitchen, limping while wiping her hands on a towel. "If it'll get him out of my gray hair for a few hours a day, he'll do it!"

Charlie rolls his eyes. "You can see who wears the trousers around here. I'll come over Wednesday and have a look-see."

"Thanks."

He hands Annie the cookie plate and starts down the hall. "Excuse me, ladies, while I get back to my honey-do list. It never ends."

After he's gone, I turn to Annie. "Terrible news about Zach."

"Yes." Annie's eyes fill with tears. "I don't understand how he got my door code. Or why he was even in the ice-cream shop. Like I told Dylan, I haven't shared my code with anyone." She waves a hand toward the living room. "Please. Come sit."

Annie leads the way to the living room. It has two walls covered from top to bottom with bookshelves, filled with the classics. There's not a television in sight, so maybe she still doesn't watch any TV. Just as she claimed back when she was my English teacher in high school.

After setting the plate on the coffee table, Annie flops into an overstuffed chair. "My joints have been acting up again lately. It's why I went home early yesterday. To think, I might have been out front serving ice cream while the murderer was in the back with Zach. I'm so glad Z or Raphe weren't hurt."

"Me too." I nod my agreement as my mind races to organize all the questions I have for Annie. I don't want to appear too obviously snoopy. "Renee said you're still close with Angelica. That you even do early readings of her books still?"

"Yes. I've read all her books before they were published. Used to be she'd send me the manuscript in the mail, but apparently, no one does that anymore. I had to finally get a laptop so she could send the books electronically. I got email too so Renee could send me the weekly work schedule. And I do love my solitaire game. I've grown to like using the computer. But you'll never see me with one of those fancy cell phones. I don't need people calling me at all hours."

Looks like Annie *could* have been hacked. "Have you noticed a big difference in the stories since Angelica started using a ghostwriter?"

Annie's eyes grow big. "Why would you think Angelica has a ghostwriter?"

Uh-oh. That must've been a secret. Or Annie hasn't figured it out yet. "Angelica's former assistant said so." No use evading the truth at this point. If Madge knows something, everyone will know soon enough.

"It's not what you think." Annie's lips compress. "Writers have slumps. That's all. Angelica just needed a little break. Clint is a very nice man, and they write the stories together. He writes the actual crime sections, and Angelica does the characterizations. I think they produce amazing work."

Apparently, Annie does know the truth. "Who usually sent you the early books? Angelica or Clint?"

"The last few years, it's been Kate. Once she got involved, I had to get the computer. She sends me books that somehow disappear off my hard drive after a month. Most of the time, they send the first half to see if I like it and then send the rest later. Not sure how that disappearing thing works, but Kate was pretty slick with things like that. She was even nice enough to send the laptop to me in return for all the reading I've done for Angelica over the years."

Now we're getting somewhere. Maybe Kate made sure she had access to all Annie's files before she sent the machine. "Did you tell Dylan, Kate sent you the computer?"

"No." Annie frowns. "Didn't see what difference that would make. But I hope he returns my laptop soon. I'm missing my solitaire!"

"If Charlie has a cellphone, I can download a free version so you can still play."

"Really? Well, that'd be just dandy of you, Sawyer. Let me go get it." Annie rises slowly from her chair and heads down the hall. "Charlie? Where's that fancy phone of yours?" she bellows as she limps away.

While Annie's gone, I send a quick text to Dylan and tell him where Annie got her computer. It seems Kate has the skills and a motive, if she figured out Zach wanted to get back together with Renee.

Annie's heavy footsteps are coming my way again, so I hit Send and then slide my phone back into my purse.

My former teacher holds out Charlie's phone. "The code is 123456. Do you think you could get me that candy-smashing game all the kids used to talk about too?"

"You got it." I smile and start the first download. "What other kinds of information does Renee email you? Besides your weekly schedule?"

"Oh, this and that." Annie drops into her soft chair again. "Little things. Like, can you fill in for Z on this date? She puts it in writing because she thinks my memory is going. But she's wrong." Annie taps her forehead. "I'm still quick as a tack."

It's *sharp* as a tack, but I'll keep that to myself.

Charlie's voice calls out from afar. "You keep forgetting to be nice to me!"

Annie waves a hand. "Ignore him. He's mad because I told him I'm not making one more meal for him until he fixes that darn washing machine. He won't let me get a new one."

"The curse of being married to a handy guy, I guess." I poke the icon to get the crushing game. "Any chance Renee might have emailed you your door code? She only installed that new time-card system and the door lock last year, right?"

"Maybe." Annie's forehead scrunches. "I don't recall if she handed me a code or sent it to me. I'm still getting used to the idea that my paycheck just shows up in my account each week. Technology these days is just fascinating."

"It is." And I'm hoping Annie has never emptied her email trash. There's probably a good chance of that if she rarely gets emails. "Speaking of amazing tech, here you go. Just tap these two buttons to start your games. I'll get out of your hair now." I hand over Charlie's phone and stand.

"So quick? Thanks, Sawyer." She takes the phone and taps the solitaire game. After she's played a few cards, she looks up. "Will I see you at the funeral? Angelica called and said it'd be the day after tomorrow. At the new parlor north of town. She said Clint, the ghostwriter, will be there too. He's handsome and single. And he has lovely hands, with the long fingers of a pianist. Might be a good match for you, if that Dylan Cooper doesn't come to his senses and beg you to take him back."

The last thing I want is to meet another man to date right now. But I do want to see who shows up at the funeral. I'm especially curious to see if Kate will show up. "I'd love to meet Clint." I grab my purse. "Don't get up. I'll see myself out."

Annie's wrinkly face lights up, and she turns to gaze out the window. "Wouldn't that be something if you married a talented writer that I introduced you to. Much better than a boy who does nothing but goofs off in my class. Nothing worse than a 'B' student capable of getting As but too lazy to do it. Dylan was even too lazy to marry you."

A slow-growing heat forms in my gut.

Shocked that Annie would say something like that, I say, "Senior year, Dylan was grieving for his mother and the demise of his parents' marriage at the same time. He needed to work things out before he committed to being a good husband to me. He feared he might be like his father, who we all know now wasn't a good husband to his mother. Dylan worked things out while serving our country in the army, and now he's keeping us all safe here. Looking back, maybe I wasn't really ready yet either."

Annie's right brow arches. "Just as I thought. You love that boy."

Charlie reappears from fixing the washing machine. "Annie, it's time for your pills. I'll see Sawyer out." He takes my arm and leads me out the front door and onto the porch. After he closes the door, he says, "Annie didn't mean anything by that. Sometimes she slips back into her teaching days. It comes and goes. You take your time and figure out what's right for both you and Dylan. Don't let anyone tell you otherwise. I'll see you Wednesday morning to give you my estimate."

Now I feel bad for getting upset with Annie.

I whisper, "She really does have a memory problem?"

Charlie nods. "Sometimes seeing former students triggers

it. Renee and I have been talking about how much longer she can work in the ice-cream shop."

"I'm so sorry to hear that." I give Charlie a hug. "She's lucky she has you to help her." After a quick squeeze, I release him and step back. "And thanks again for considering my home repair project. See you Wednesday."

"You will." Charlie turns and goes back inside.

Sad, that. But now I'm not sure if it was Kate who sent Annie the computer or not. It could just as easily have been sent by Angelica.

I turn around to head home and almost crash into Dylan. "Oh. Hi."

He gently takes my arm much like Charlie just did and leads me down the driveway. When we hit the sidewalk, Dylan says, "I draw the line at you interrogating key players in my case."

"I was bribing Charlie with cookies to work on my house. Annie just happened to be there too."

Dylan's only response is a clenched jaw.

I continue, "The good news is, Brittany's cookies worked, and Charlie's coming by to give me an estimate. But I didn't know Annie had memory problems, so that text I sent you might not be correct about Annie's computer."

"That's why I just texted Charlie to confirm." Dylan tugs on my arm to stop walking and faces me. "No more, Sawyer. You will not speak to any more of Renee's employees about Zach's death. Is that clear?"

Z and Raphe were the two I was planning to drop in on

next. "Speaking of them, do their stories match the camera's footage?"

Dylan crosses his arms. "Have you seen me make any arrests?"

"Okay. Then they match and they aren't suspects. So, what did Charlie say? Did Kate really send Annie the computer?"

The vein in Dylan's forehead that bulges when he's furious is making an appearance, so I better tread lightly.

"You know what?" He runs a hand down his face to calm himself. "I think we should take our no-talking-about-Renee rule one step further. I think you and I shouldn't speak at all until I solve this case. Without any help from you!"

I want to yell back. Instead, I take a second and then calmly reply, "Renee is being framed. She needs all the help she can get. No matter where she gets it."

He leans closer. "You could be killed too, if the murderer thinks you're involved. You need to stay out of this."

Does Dylan even know me? I've never backed away from helping a friend. "I can't just stop caring about her."

"Really? You've done a great job not caring about me for eight long years." He steps around me and walks away.

I'm not going to take that sitting down. I catch up and grab his arm to stop him. "Wait a minute. Who left whom again?"

Dylan says, "I told you I needed time to get my head on straight. I never said I didn't love you anymore." He stares intently into my eyes. "You made that assumption all on your own and quit taking my calls. Just like you might make some bad assumptions about this case that could get you killed. So. Back. Off." He turns and crosses the street.

"Dylan. Wait."

I start after him, but he keeps walking, raising a hand to signal he's done with our conversation.

And maybe done with me as well.

CHAPTER 8

*A*fter my dressing down from Dylan, I flop onto a
stool at my kitchen counter as sounds of a muted
conversation drift from the living room. Gage and Renee
must be strategizing about her case.

I regret making Dylan angry earlier, but at the same time,
I'm warring with my overwhelming need to help Renee. She
and I vowed as children to always have the other's back, and
I intend to honor that promise.

Taking stock of what I know so far about Renee's case,
Raphe's hacking skills—that he's shown he's not afraid to use
—still bother me. Is it a coincidence that we have Raphe the
hacker and technophobe Annie, whose door code was used,
both working in the same shop where Zach was killed? I
doubt it. We really need to find a computer expert tomorrow
to help prove that.

And I need to insist that Brittany talk to Dylan. She'll be mad at me, but I think Dylan needs to know what we know about Raphe.

Gage appears and sits beside me. "Hi. Why the frown?"

"Just thinking." I don't want to talk about my fight with Dylan. "Where's Renee?"

"Taking a shower. Dylan wants us to come to the station and answer a few more questions."

That can't be good. Dylan probably wants to talk about Mr. Martinez's claims of seeing Renee go into her store yesterday afternoon. Which, according to Madge, could lead to Renee's arrest. "Did Brittany or Renee talk to you about Raphe's hacking?"

"Yes." Gage stands and pours us both cups of coffee. "I asked Brittany to talk to Dylan, but she said that Raphe didn't do anything wrong. Worse, if she tells on him, it will ruin *everything*. Whatever *everything* involves."

"Raphe is her first crush. He's the most important thing in her world right now. Even though we both know nothing will probably ever come of their little romance."

"Oh, I don't know." Gage's green eyes twinkle. "You were my first crush. And we're still exploring that."

"True." But it's hard to focus on that at the moment. "I stand corrected."

He grins and slips a steaming mug of coffee in front of me. "What did you learn from Mr. Martinez and Annie?"

"A lot, actually." I relay the conversations, and just when I'm about finished recapping my morning sleuthing, Brittany joins us in the kitchen, so I stop talking.

After rummaging through the fridge for lunch options and finally choosing leftover pizza, she looks up and sees us both watching her. "What?"

This is where I need to get brave. Just like I promised Madge. Be tough. Be a parent— sort of.

I add as much authority to my voice as I can muster. "After you're done eating, you and I need to go talk to Dylan about Raphe."

Brittany's jaw drops. "But you promised. You said you'd keep my secret!" She tosses the plastic zip bag with the pizza onto the counter so she can dramatically cross her arms. Her stare, filled with betrayal, pokes at my heart.

"Technically, I never promised you that. I've been giving it a lot of thought, and I think for Renee's sake, you need to come clean. You can tell Raphe I made you." That sounded like something my parents might have said. But my dad is a traveling magician who never disciplined me, and my mom was a hippie who rarely corrected me, so I'm not sure my response was strong enough.

"I'm not doing it." Brittany lifts her chin. "I was fine before you showed up. And I can be fine again without you. I'll just go pack my things."

Panic sets in as I glance at Gage for some guidance. He nods to keep me going.

I don't want Brittany to walk out the door and disappear the way her mother is famous for. Brittany can hate me, but I can't let her do something that would put her in danger. "You need a guardian, or you'll be sent to foster care. And I'm all you have at the moment. You can be mad at me for trying to save my best friend later."

Brittany's eyes fill with angry tears as she stares at me. "You're saying Renee is more important than me?"

"No. I'm saying it's the right thing to do. We'll let Dylan decide what he'll do with the information we give him."

"Raphe will *hate* me." Tears have escaped and are slipping down Brittany's cheeks.

Trying my best to ignore the way her tears stab at my heart, I say, "Not if you explain Renee's situation. She's been a good friend to you too. And not if he's the kind of guy who's good enough to date *you.*"

As Brittany frowns and stews, I'm holding my breath, hoping with all my heart she doesn't run. My mom trusted me to take care of Brittany. I don't want to disrespect my mother's dying wishes. "Besides, I'd miss you too much if you left. So please don't do that."

Brittany's bottom lip trembles as she continues to stare at me. Finally, she says, "Fine," throws her hands up in defeat, and marches toward the back door. "Let's get this over with, then."

Relieved, I let out a long breath and follow behind Brittany's retreating figure that's already out the door. I say to Gage, "Lock up when you guys leave."

Gage calls out, "Sawyer?"

I pop my head back inside the doorway. "Yes?"

"I'll be the villain and call Dylan now to express my concerns about Raphe. You can tell Brittany you knew I was going to do it." He smiles sweetly at me. "That was nicely done with her, by the way."

"Thank you." His kind words make my heart swell with… something. I'll have to think about it later, though, because now I'm going to have to face a potentially very angry Dylan when he finds out I didn't tell him about Raphe right away. It makes my stomach ache.

After catching up with Brittany, we walk in deafening silence to the station.

Great. Dylan's not speaking to me, and now neither is Brittany. I want to reason with her, but maybe it's best to let her stew for a while. And while I appreciate Gage's offer to be the bad guy, I won't take him up on it. Brittany needs a guardian who will guide her more than she needs a friend in me. We'll both have to figure out our relationship as we go.

My phone rings, diverting my attention from all those ignoring me. It's my sister, Megan. "Hey, Megs. I've meant to call you. I really need your help with something." I want to ask about Brittany dating, but I can't do it in front of her. "Can I call you back in an hour or so?"

"Sure. I'm in the ER with Collin. He hurt his arm skateboarding. It looks broken to me, but brains are my specialty, not bones, so we're waiting for an X-ray. I tried to call Dylan to let him know we might be a little late for the barbecue this afternoon, but he hasn't called back. Will you let him know for us?"

"Will do." I'd completely forgotten about Sunday dinner at Dylan's for my brother-in-law's birthday. "Tell Collin anyone with broken bones deserves two desserts tonight. Keep me posted."

"Yep." My always-busy sister hangs up.

"Goodbye to you too," I say and disconnect, while pondering if I'm even still invited to Dylan's for his brother Lance's birthday party. My dad is supposed to make an appearance too, but we never set him a place until we see the whites of his eyes. Max the Magnificent is the definition of flaky, but we love him anyway.

And this is why having a romantic relationship with Dylan gets complicated. If we want to see our family, sometimes we'll have to see each other as well. Whether we're on speaking terms or not.

While we climb the steps to the municipal building, Brittany says quietly, "What did Collin break?"

"Potentially his arm. You might have to go to Lance's birthday party without me this afternoon. Dylan's mad at me for snooping around in Renee's case." Brittany likes Megan's kids Collin and Alexandra. They're already like younger cousins to her. And she adores my father. Brittany had been looking forward to seeing everyone today.

She says, "It's not like Dylan can just uninvite you to the birthday party. Can he?"

I let out a long sigh. "We'll see, I guess." I tug on the glass door and wait for Brittany to pass by first, and then I follow her down the hall to the station.

Madge is on the phone as usual, but sees us and points to Dylan's office, effectively giving us the go-ahead, so we change direction. Dylan is standing with his back to us, hands flexing at his sides, staring out the window. Part of me wants to turn around and let him calm down a bit after our disagreement, and the other part wants to get this over with.

I clear the apprehension from my throat. "Hi. Brittany has something she wants to tell you. If you don't need me, I'll wait outside."

Dylan turns and addresses Brittany. "Since you're a minor, I'd like Sawyer here too." Dylan motions to the guest chairs in front of his desk and then sits in his big leather chair.

Brittany flops dramatically into her seat. "Raphe doesn't have anything to do with Zach's death. I'm only doing this because she's making me."

Dylan nods and takes out a legal pad. "Gage filled me in, but I'd like you to tell me in your own words." Dylan's gaze stays firmly on Brittany.

That he won't look at me makes me even sicker to my stomach. I hate arguing with him. Technically, I still don't think I did anything wrong, but I'll do as he asks, and stay away from Z and Raphe. But I can't stop helping Renee.

While Brittany tells Dylan about Raphe hacking fellow game players, I sink into the other chair, recapping in my mind what Mr. Martinez said earlier. Renee never stuffs her long hair under baseball caps. I'm not even sure it'd fit. Maybe I'll ask her to try that when I get home. Not that I have a baseball cap. Maybe I can borrow one from Dylan or Gage.

As Brittany reluctantly drones on, I rewind all the things Mr. Martinez mentioned. About taking his pills at the same time each day, and about him seeing Renee's fancy watch when she punched in the code with her right hand. Even though she's left-handed.

Something about that watch niggles at my brain. What were all the things Renee told me it could do? A thought strikes, and I blurt out, "Do you have Renee's watch?"

Dylan and Brittany both turn and look at me like I've lost a screw. Dylan says, "I'd like to finish—"

I lean forward and lay my hand on Dylan's arm. "You don't understand. Renee's watch has GPS. It keeps track of her rides. That's how we can prove she wasn't here at the time of Zach's murder!" Joy fills me at the prospect of proving Renee innocent.

"Let me see." Dylan riffles through a stack of papers and studies one. Slowly, he shakes his head. "She wasn't wearing a watch when we picked her up. I'll be sure to ask her about that when she comes in."

What? Renee always tracks her rides. She's trying to beat the miles she rode last year. "Are you sure?"

Dylan nods at the paper in his hands and then turns his attention back to Brittany.

Why wasn't Renee wearing the watch? She always wears it. Doubt about her story wants to creep in, but I'm not going to let it. I *know* Renee. She did not kill Zach. Whoever is framing her is doing a bang-up job, though.

After Brittany is finished, Dylan sets his pen down and crosses his arms. He finally looks me straight in the eyes. "Anything else you're keeping from me?"

Before I can answer, Brittany stands and says, "The only thing she's keeping from you is that she obviously still loves you. I wish you guys would just work it out and be done with it!" Brittany stomps toward the office door and snaps it closed behind her.

Yikes. I've just found a new definition for awkward.

After we sit in stunned silence for what feels like a full minute, Dylan finally says, "If only it were that simple."

I can only nod because there's a big lump in my throat. I'm grateful he understands. And maybe I misunderstood his motives for calling off the wedding. After all, the prospect of marrying me had to be less scary than the idea of getting shot at in the army. I hope.

"Hey." Dylan reaches across his desk and takes my hand. "I'm sorry I lost my temper earlier. I'm seriously worried about your safety. That's why I think we should keep our distance until this case is solved. I didn't mean to rehash all the other stuff."

I clear the boulder from my throat and whisper, "Maybe we *should* rehash—"

A knock on the door interrupts me before Madge's head pops inside. "Gage and Renee are here to see you."

"Send them in, please." Dylan gives my hand, still

encased in his, a squeeze. "Meg just called. Collin broke his arm, and I'm buried up to my eyeballs in this case, so I postponed Lance's party. Tell your dad I'm sorry to miss him."

I guess Dylan isn't interested in rehashing our past after all. Or maybe he doesn't want Madge to hear us talking about it. "I'll pass on your regret to my dad. I'm sure you'll both be heartbroken." My father still can't forgive Dylan for leaving me at the altar.

Dylan takes his hand from mine and lays it over his heart. "Shattered."

I'm just about to comment on what a smart aleck Dylan is when Renee and Gage pass through the open door.

This is my chance to find out about the watch directly, so I turn to Renee, "Did you have your smartwatch on yesterday to track your miles? And location?"

"Yes!" Renee nods enthusiastically, obviously understanding the importance of that data, but then her expression dims, and she turns to Dylan. "But it won't do any good. The watch was smashed to bits when I fell. There was no saving it. I was hurt and angry, so I tossed it into a trash bin in the parking lot at the base of the trail."

"The data should still be trackable, but I'd like to verify the watch's location. It's the weekend. Maybe it's not too late to find it." Dylan punches a button on his desk phone. "Find out when they pick up the trash on the bike trail Renee was on." He hangs up and points a finger at me. "No dumpster diving, Sawyer. I'll send one of my deputies."

Dylan knows me too well. I was almost out the door and on my way. "Fine. And you're welcome, by the way."

"Let's hope we can find it." Dylan motions to Renee and Gage. "Have a seat, guys. Sawyer was just leaving."

Soundly dismissed, I can't help saying, "You're welcome, anyway," as I close the door behind me.

I make my way to Madge's desk to see if there's anything new she can tell me.

Madge waits until I settle into her guest chair before she blurts, "Guess who's coming to the funeral on Tuesday?"

She's probably going to tell me about Angelica's ghost-writer, Clint, but I'll play along. "Who?"

"Kate, Angelica's former assistant. She told one of the deputies that she has a theory about who the murderer is but didn't want to discuss it over the phone. Says she ran some fancy program that searches her computer for intrusions, and get this. She claims all her electronics were hacked!"

Right. Says Kate, who probably hacked Annie's computer before she sent it to my former teacher. Maybe she's trying to cover her tracks. "When does she arrive?"

"Tomorrow at three. Dylan is picking her up himself. Guess he doesn't trust any of his deputies not to drool on her on the way back here."

"Drool on her?"

Madge nods as she taps keys on her computer. "A little research showed Ms. Kate dresses conservatively when working, but her so-called private social media proves she's quite the vixen after hours." Madge turns her screen so I can see. "Kate claims these pics were from a Halloween party a few years ago that someone hacked from her phone. What do you think?"

The screen shows pictures of a blonde bombshell dressed in very little leather. "I think Kate must've won the best costume prize that year. That whip looks like the real deal. And those chains… I'm not even sure what a person would do with those."

"It just looks painful to me." Madge smiles as she turns her screen back around. "But the guys in the office were sure eager to draw straws to see who'd pick her up. Until Dylan got wind of it and shut down their game. He said he'd do the deed himself."

"How noble of him," I say dryly. "Gotta run. Keep me in the loop."

"Is that a pang of jealousy I detect in your tone?" Madge can barely contain her smirk.

"No, that's impatience to get Renee off the hook." I stand to leave. "Dylan's decided he and I aren't speaking right now anyway."

"Wait." Madge grabs my hand to stop me. "If it makes you feel any better, everyone around here would like you guys to work things out. We're hoping it'll make Dylan less agitated. He hasn't been the same since you came back to town."

I slowly sink back into my chair. "I'm making him miserable?" That's the last thing I'd want to do to anyone.

"No, honey." Madge shakes her head. "You reminded him that he's not happy. He'd been filling his spare time building his new house outside town, but he can't even find joy in that since you've been back."

That must be the house from the plans I'd accidentally seen in his office a few weeks ago. "So instead of having a real conversation with me, he asks me to date Gage? That makes no sense."

"Since when does love make sense?" Madge waves a hand. "But if you ask me, maybe it wasn't such a dumb idea. His challenge has clearly been in the back of your mind since he suggested it yesterday. Which I suspect was his sneaky plan all along."

"Yeah, that's my guess too." I want to ask Madge's advice. She's the motherly type, so it's almost impossible not to. It's her superpower. That, and being nosy, which has been quite beneficial to me of late.

On the other hand, she loves Dylan and is biased. I suspect Dylan and Madge concocted his little plan together. "Well then, maybe I'll invite Gage to dinner tonight. It'll make Dylan happy again."

Madge's smug expression quickly dissipates. "Hold up. I'm not sure that's the answer."

"I think it's the *only* way to find the answer. I'll see you later." I turn and head for the office door while Madge sputters behind me. It's the first time I've ever seen her speechless.

It makes me smile.

When I tug on the heavy door to open it, I nearly run into a blonde woman dressed as a sexy, built librarian. Kate, in the flesh, rushes past me and heads for Madge's desk, leaving behind a trail of flowery perfume that makes me want to sneeze.

Madge and I lock gazes. I'm pretty sure Madge is thinking the same thing I am. There's no way Kate could've gotten to California that fast from Florida where she claimed to be when the deputy spoke to her this morning.

It seems Kate was nearby at the time of Zach's death after all.

CHAPTER 9

I'm making dinner while waiting for Madge to call. I've been dying to hear how Kate made it to Sunset Cove so fast, and why she lied to the deputy about where she was and when she'd arrive. I'm restraining from calling Madge because I have a houseful of starving people I need to feed, myself included. I haven't eaten since breakfast. I'll call Madge after dinner.

Added to the hungry brood already here, I invited the Admiral to join us when I ran into him at the grocery store earlier. He's a member of our book club and my mom's former...something. I still haven't totally figured out what their relationship had been. Other than a secret from only me, apparently. On the other hand, my parents never married, so I don't know why I would expect a conventional relationship from my mom anyway. The Admiral is also an amateur sleuth, so he might come in handy to help solve Renee's case.

The adults are sipping an excellent red wine in the living room, waiting for my lasagna to get bubbly and happy. Cooper has joined them, hoping for crumbs from the appetizers, and Brittany is pouting in the nook, pretending not to watch me cook. "Want to slice the bread, Brittany? Then you can spread the garlic butter on top."

She huffs out a breath in protest but slides out of the nook to help. She's still upset with me but appears to be thawing a bit.

Brittany gets busy but makes me cringe by the way she's using the knife. "It's safer if you tuck your fingers in on your left hand. And then lead with your knuckles. Can I show you?" I slice a piece of bread and then hand the knife back. "See? Easy-peasy."

Brittany nods and goes back to the way she was cutting before. I can't watch, so I start on the salad.

While I'm tossing the romaine with my signature red wine vinaigrette, one I plan to serve at my new restaurant once it's built, there's a knock on my back door. I wipe my hands on the towel tucked at my waist and take a peek outside. It's my dad looking dapper in one of the two black suits he wears for his magic shows. His dark hair has dramatic white streaks at the temples his hairdresser has added since I can remember. He thinks it makes him look exotic and regal on stage. I think it makes him look like a vampire from those old black-and-white movies. Especially when he's in full makeup. From the leftover eyeliner, I can tell he's just come from a recent performance.

I open the door and hold out my arms for a hug. "You're early. The party started at five, and it's only seven." My dad will be late for his own funeral. How he manages to be on time for his magic shows stumps us all.

My father wraps me up in a bear hug. "Nice to see you too, Jellybean."

He knows I hate that nickname. I guess I deserved that for teasing him. "Come in, Count Dracula."

Brittany pauses in her butchering of the bread. "You do look a little like a vampire, Max. But in a good way."

My good-natured dad grins, exposing his startling white caps, and gives Brittany a quick hug too. "It's why I'm late. I can't go out into direct sunlight. What smells so heavenly?"

Brittany says, "*Jellybean* is making lasagna that's taking *forever* to cook." She glances at me and smirks.

I have a feeling it's not the last I'll hear my dreaded nickname from her.

My dad pours himself a glass of wine and lifts it. "All good things are worth the wait. Or is that all good things come to an end?" He looks at me. "You've got a few fancy degrees, Sawyer. How does that saying go again?"

My dad still thinks I've wasted my talents by not using my advanced engineering degree from MIT. He cringed when I told him I was going to culinary school after spending a few years at an engineering job I hated. But he likes my cooking.

"I've read a few variations of that saying." I top off the salad with shaved parmesan. "But Mark Twain said, 'All good things arrive unto them that wait—and don't die in the meantime.'"

Brittany frowns. "Is that even proper English?"

My dad laughs. "I was thinking the same."

When Brittany yelps in pain, my dad's face turns white. He grips the island to keep himself upright. "Blood. Oh my. There's blood, Sawyer."

Brittany has nicked her finger. I hate blood too, it makes my head go all woozy, but I'm more worried about my dad passing out, as he's prone to do.

I toss a clean towel to Brittany and then grab my dad's arm to lead him to the nook. "It's just a little cut, Dad. No big deal." But my stomach has just turned over in revulsion too. I barely passed the butchering classes while I was in culinary school.

My father's eyes are fluttering, so I push his head between his knees. "Deep breaths, Dad."

When another knock sounds on the door, I don't know what to do. I can't leave my dad quite yet, and Brittany is busy washing off blood in the sink, so I call out, "Come in! It's open."

The door creaks, and Dylan's head appears. When he sees my dad, Dylan stops dead in his tracks. "Hi. I wanted to talk to Renee, but I'll just... Go."

At the sound of Dylan's voice, my father's head pops

straight up. "Well, if it isn't the ghostly groom. Come in, and I'll make you disappear all over again."

"Dad. Please." I close my eyes and count to five. "Come in, Dylan. You can check on Brittany's wound over there while I escort my father to the living room to join the others." I tug on my father's arm. "Let's go, Count. Away from all this tempting blood."

My dad glares at Dylan before letting me pull him toward the living room. Then he says, loudly, "For the record, I like that Gage fellow much better than that sheriff."

"Yes, I know." I stop walking and stare into my dad's pretty blue eyes. "What I don't understand is why, if I've forgiven Dylan for leaving me at the altar, can't you?"

My dad whispers, "Because he hurt you. And that will always slay me." My father lays a quick kiss on my forehead. "Besides, do you know how many rabbits I had to pull out of my hat to pay for that shindig that never happened?"

"Seriously? I'm sure Dylan would write you a check if that'd help you move on."

"That's the best idea I've heard all day. And I'm fine now. Thank you." My dad dramatically bows before he turns and starts down the long hall toward the living room. When he's almost there, he calls out, "I'll have to look for that receipt!"

Shaking my head, I return to the kitchen to see about Dylan.

He's busy earnestly dressing Brittany's little cut with a bandage. He says, "Sometimes nicks and paper cuts hurt worse than a deep slice." Dylan finishes up his handiwork and takes a step back. "There. Good as new."

"Gee, thanks, Dad." Brittany holds up her injured finger. "Are you going to kiss it now too?"

Dylan sputters and turns three shades of red.

His total mortification is sweet and makes me a whole lot less angry at him for being mad at me. "Stop teasing him, Brittany." I swat her with my towel and then turn to Dylan. "Want me to have Renee call you when we're done with dinner?"

Dylan's gaze drops to his shoes as he shoves his hands into his pockets. "I'll talk to Renee tomorrow. Just wanted to tell her we found the broken watch in the trash." He clears his throat and then meets my curious stare. "You said maybe we should rehash things. But you're busy. We can do it later."

"Right now works." I grab Dylan's hand and lead him to the backyard. After the door closes behind us and we're alone, I say, "Let me guess. You're really here because Madge spilled about me inviting Gage to dinner tonight. Right?"

Dylan nods. "I wanted to tell you something. Before it's too late."

I withhold a sigh. "This isn't a romantic dinner. There are four others here too. Have you changed your mind about wanting me to date Gage?"

"No." Dylan winces. "You should explore that. You said you'd like to take a hiatus from dating—me. And I need to respect that."

Words straight out of Madge's mouth, if I had to guess.

"But you'd still like to talk about what happened on our nonwedding day? Even though you decided we're not speaking right now because of the case? You're confusing me."

"Sorry." Dylan sucks in a deep breath. "I was trying to give you some space after your mom's death. But then when Gage entered the picture, I worried I'd lose..." Dylan lays his hands on my arms. "When I saw you after all those years at your mom's funeral, I just wanted to hug you and never let go. Just being in the same room as you made me feel alive again. But I'd hurt you and earned every ounce of your anger. It was selfish of me to run off and lick my wounds alone. I'll always be sorry for that. And for hurting you, Sawyer."

Finally! A real apology.

"Thank you. But I wish you could've said all this at Meg and Lance's wedding. You didn't speak to me at all that day." I wrap my arms around him and hold him tight because I do appreciate the apology. "It broke my heart all over again."

"I was afraid I'd lose it if I spoke to you that day. And I had to be Lance's best man." He tucks his face in the crook of my neck and whispers, "Your mom said I made you cry. I hated myself even more for that. You never cry."

I sometimes do, but it's rare. "What do you want from me now?"

"I'd appreciate a second chance. To date you. A fresh start, like it's brand-new, and see where it goes from there. Whenever—or if ever—you feel ready. I realize you might want to explore other options, and I respect that. My offer won't expire."

Never expire?

That makes my heart melt. The same heart I had to put back together again after he shattered it. Can't be too quick to forget that. "Thank you. I know that was hard. You hate talking about feelings. Especially yours."

"I really do." He leans away but keeps his hands on my waist. "Should I ask how you're feeling, or give you a rain check?"

"I'll take a rain check." That he realizes I can't instantly forgive someone who hurt me so deeply gives me hope for our future. He's changed a lot in our years apart. All for the better from what I've seen in the last few months. "But what about the case? Are we talking about that or not? Because I have some questions."

"Of course you do." A slow grin lights his face. "I've thought a few times I should deputize you. Then I can legally use that curious nature of yours."

I nod enthusiastically. "I think that's a great idea."

"But then you'd have to actually listen to me and obey commands." His brows lift in challenge.

"Well, forget it, then. Do you want to stay for dinner? There's plenty." It could be awkward with my dad and Gage, but we're all adults.

"I'd love to stay. But better not. Shouldn't be fraternizing with my prime suspect and her lawyer. Especially if I have to make an arrest."

"Arrest?" My stomach drops. "Did Kate tell you something tonight to implicate Renee further?"

Dylan nods as he steps away from me, his expression grim, effectively rebuilding that invisible barrier he's been putting between us. "There's too much evidence to ignore. I've got one more thing to check out in the morning. And I'll send Renee's watch to the crime lab in the city to see if we can salvage something. But they're pretty backed up, so it could take a while. Night, Sawyer." He turns and walks away.

Oh boy. It looks like we need that computer expert now —no time to wait until morning. Maybe the Admiral knows someone who can help us.

Turning on my heel, I hightail back into the kitchen where Brittany is removing the lasagna from the oven. In the time I was outside, Brittany has laid all the food out buffet style, even adding nicely folded cloth napkins around silverware sets as I'd have done. She's poured pitchers of water and tea and set out cookies on trays for dessert. All the dressing options surround the salad bowl and plates, and she even found the cracked pepper mill. The kid has been paying more attention in the kitchen while I worked than I realized.

I set my hands on my hips. "Nice job, Brit. I'm impressed."

She glances over her shoulder. "'Bout time you're back. Everyone is starving. Are you two engaged now or what?"

"None of your business." But after talking to Dylan, I now know there are still issues that have to be resolved before I move on—if I move on—so I should talk to Gage as soon as I can. I don't want to string him along.

Brittany sets the hot pan on the granite island next to her toasty garlic bread. "Well, not to be a jerk or anything, but I think I should mention that your best friend is moving in on your option two. So maybe you should just take Dylan back and be done with it."

"My option two?"

She nods. "Watch the way Gage and Renee look at each other. It's been going on the whole time she's been staying here."

I can't help but straighten the crooked plates a tad as I say, "Maybe you're mistaking gratitude and frustration with her case for attraction? Renee needs Gage's help desperately right now."

Brittany shakes her head as she tugs off the oven gloves. "My mom always said men love to be needed. Fake that and he's all yours. That's how she got the occasional rich ones. If only for a while. But you and I? We're stronger than that. We don't need anyone, do we, Sawyer?"

Don't need anyone?

I'm not that independent. Am I?

Maybe a little. Growing up with irresponsible, but kind, parents makes a gal have to figure out life on her own.

It stings a bit to acknowledge it. Especially coming from a fifteen-year-old.

Before I can reply, the Admiral, tall, white-haired, and wearing his trusty cardigan even though it's warm out, enters the kitchen. "This mess hall smells fantastic, Sailor. When do we eat?"

"It's all ready. Please, serve yourself." I turn to Brittany. "Will you ask everyone to grab their plates?"

"Yeah. But just watch those two at dinner. You'll see." She heads out to gather everyone. Before she's out the door, she says, "And we all call Sawyer *Jellybean* around here, Admiral."

"Really?" The Admiral's bushy white brows hop up, and his gaze finds mine. "Your mother never mentioned that. I'll take note."

He'll most likely never remember, so I'll let Brittany get away with that just this once. Taking an opportunity while we're alone, I ask, "Admiral? Is there someone in town we can trust who has exceptional computer skills? Someone familiar with hacking. To help Renee?"

The Admiral heaps his plate with lasagna. "Nick, the new guy in book club, works in the IT department for the mayor. He seems a bright lad."

"I don't want someone who works for my uncle. Anyone else?" My uncle probably sent Nick to join the club to keep tabs on my bookstore and me. Uncle Frank is waiting for the bookstore to fail and for me to move away. That way, the assets in my inherited trust all go to him. But he'd actually be able to sell them and liquidate, unlike me.

Admiral Wright bites into a cookie. "Can't think of anyone else. Nick's single and your age. Bet if you invited him for dinner, he'd be here in a flash."

"Maybe I'll let Renee decide." I don't want to invite a spy into our midst, but we need help.

"Up to you. This all looks grand, Sawyer." The Admiral takes his plate and heads to the dining room.

After everyone is seated in the huge wallpapered and wainscoted dining room that seats twenty, I tug the towel from my waistband, fill my plate, and join everyone at the table. We rarely used this room filled with antique table, chairs, and sideboards that are showing their age, after my grandparents died. But it could be beautiful again. Maybe I'll ask Annie's husband to start the rehab in here after we fix the more pressing rotted-wood problems.

Cooper snuggles between my feet and yawns, the little social butterfly. He wore himself out, flitting from person to person, happily receiving any rubs he could while batting his long lashes in hopes for scraps. But he'll dump me again like a load of gravel if anyone drops some food, the traitor.

I take a bite of the warm, garlicky bread, while Renee and Gage fill my dad and the Admiral in on all the specifics of the case.

After I swallow, I say, "I forgot to tell you guys. Dylan said they found the watch in the trash bin. He's sending it to a lab in the city."

Renee reaches out and grabs Gage's hand, squeezing it. "This might be the break we needed. You were right, Gage. I should've listened."

Gage's green eyes go all soft and gooey in a way he's never looked at me. "The truth always prevails." He stares into Renee's eyes with a goofy little grin on his face.

Huh. Maybe Brittany's right about those two.

Renee doesn't usually commit to men. She plays with them until she gets bored and then sends them packing. In a kind way. Gage knows that. Everyone does. Maybe this time, she genuinely has feelings. And who could blame Gage? Renee's not only pretty, she's a great friend.

I should feel a little jealous, but I don't feel even a twinge of…anything.

Just as I tune back in to the table's discussion, my dad says, "Now where did my napkin go? Ah. Here it is." It suddenly appears, seemingly out of thin air, delighting everyone else at the table.

I glance at Brittany, and we both smile. We've seen that trick one too many times.

The Admiral says, "If only you could make Renee's problems disappear so easily, Max. What we really need is Nick's computer expertise, don't you agree, Renee?"

Renee nods. "But would whatever we find be admissible in court?"

That's a good question. One I hadn't considered. Could we do more harm than good if we hire our own hacker? I glance at Gage. "Should we try to find out what we can on our own or not?"

My dad interjects, "What you need is someone in the know. A plant. Like I often have in my audiences during my magic shows."

The Admiral sits back in his chair and smiles. "Yes, I think that's the perfect battle strategy."

Oh no. Here we go. "Dad. I don't think—"

A NOVEL WAY TO DIE

My dad holds up a hand. "Wait, Jellybean. I have an amazing plan."

I want to groan. Not for the jellybean comment, but because my father isn't the best magician in the world and often relies on a few "gray areas" of magic to make his shows realistic. I want to save him the embarrassment of that reveal, but everyone at the table is a friend. I'm probably just being overprotective of him. "Sorry to interrupt. What's your idea?"

Still basking at the center of attention, my dad says, "What I do is very similar to what someone is doing to you, Renee."

"How so?" Renee, always a fan of my dad's, sets her fork down and gives Max her total attention.

"Someone—the murderer in this case—is using the power of suggestion and distraction. Tools every good magician uses. They make you look guilty while they get away with murder."

The Admiral says, "Yes. A Trojan horse tactic, so to speak. Something pretty and distracting, but with bad intentions inside."

Bemused, Gage asks, "So how do we get the murderer to reveal their tricks, Max?"

My father replies, "When performing my mind-reading tricks, I always choose the most innocent-looking sorts from the audience, people who look trustworthy. I ask them to reveal something unique about themselves, then I slip them some cash and let them know that they can keep it or donate it to help the kids with cancer I invite to every show. No one ever keeps it, so donations to a great cause occur, my tricks go off without a hitch, and everyone goes home happy and amazed. It's a win-win."

Gage frowns. "Who would we bribe to help us in this case? I'm not following."

"Who here looks the most innocuous among us?" My dad waves a hand to include the entire table. "Dare I say childlike and innocent. Someone who could blend into the hacker crowd, find out what we need, and point that unreliable sheriff in the right direction without him even knowing?"

I'm totally confused by what my father is saying. "Just spit it out, Dad."

"It's the same person who has just slipped from the room while all eyes were on me."

Stunned, I do a quick head count. "No way I'm involving Brittany. She's just a kid."

My dad lifts a finger. "A kid who is wise beyond her years. Who managed to live in this small town for a long time without a parent, and nobody knew it. Someone who was caught hacking by your mother and given a choice. To clean up her act and live with Zoe or be turned over to the authorities."

"That's right!" The Admiral sits up straighter. "I'd forgotten about that. Zoe happened upon Brittany's antics at the bookstore one day. Brittany most likely would've never been caught otherwise. She'd been running a flimflam for years. She's good, Sawyer. And loyal, as well as motivated to stay under the radar because your mother has all the evidence against Brittany. The perfect operative. Use her."

My jaw drops while my brain tries to catch up. It was bad enough that before my mom died, she forgot to tell me I was going to be in charge of a fifteen-year-old. Didn't even bother to mention she'd been seeing the Admiral for years. And that I had to search high and low for her secret stash of expensive wine before the bad guys got it, or I'd never be able to finance my future restaurant.

But now it seems my mom forgot to tell me one other small detail. That I'm the guardian of a reformed criminal. But where on earth is the evidence? I've already turned the house upside down when looking for the other things she hid for me.

What other surprises am I going to uncover next? And what kind of grift had Brittany been running?

CHAPTER 10

*A*fter my dad and the Admiral have left, Renee and Gage insist on dish duty—something I'll never argue against. Cooper joins them in hopes of more leftovers "accidentally" falling his way.

I take the opportunity to go upstairs and talk to Brittany. I knock on her door, but there's no answer. Hopefully, my dad exposing her secret hasn't made her decide to leave.

I knock again, this time louder.

Still no response, so I try the knob, and it's locked. Well, as secured as a door can be in this old house. I run to my room down the hall and grab a bobby pin from the little box my mom always kept on her dressing table. I perfected this lock-picking technique when my sister and I were kids.

After I wiggle the straightened pin to the right and then jiggle it a tad to the left, the knob finally turns. I poke my head inside Brittany's bedroom. Clothes are strewn all over the place, and her backpack is stuffed to the brim. But she hasn't gone anywhere. She's lying on the bed with her eyes closed, listening to whatever is streaming through her headphones. I clear my throat and call out as loudly as I can, "Can we talk, please?"

One of Brittany's eyes pops open. "Breaking and entering is illegal, you know."

"Not in my own home." I cross the room and sit on the side of the bed. "You're packed. Where are you planning to go?"

"Nowhere. I changed my mind."

Thank goodness! "Smart move. So, what did my mom catch you doing online?"

"Scamming creepy men." Brittany tugs off her headphones. "After they'd fall for a story and send money, thinking they'd get something else in return, I'd ghost them. They'd never turn me in, because they knew they were doing something wrong. I'm not proud of it, but I needed to survive."

I want to shake Brittany's mother every time I hear how she mistreated her daughter. Who leaves a kid to survive on their own like that?

My mom gave Brittany a job after school because she felt sorry for her. Not because she could afford the help. "Are you still doing that? Scamming men for money? Or anything else illegal?" I hold my breath and hope she's not, or I don't know what I'll do.

"No." She meets my gaze. "I promised your mom I'd stop. But I've been tempted. It sucks not having enough money for new clothes and stuff. School starts in a few weeks."

How could I have forgotten that? I can't pay Brittany as much as I'd like to at the bookstore. It barely turns a profit most months. But because my mom legally adopted Brittany, she can use some of the trust money, to my uncle's undying chagrin, but only for health and education needs. I don't think school clothes count, or my sister and I would have had the best, like the education we both got at top colleges. "No worries. I'll sell a bottle of Mom's wine, and we'll go shopping. Maybe we can go to the city and have lunch. Make a day of it?" The rare wine sells for thousands a bottle. I've never even been tempted to taste it. I'd rather have the money collectors are willing to pay.

Brittany shrugs. "Your mom left all that wine to fund your restaurant. Are you sure?"

"Absolutely. We'll invite Renee too because she has better fashion sense than both of us combined. But she won't be able to come if we don't prove she's innocent. Can you help us figure this all out?"

"Maybe." Brittany sits up, draws her knees against her chest, and wraps her arms around them. "Most likely, every- thing we need is stored in the cloud, assuming she didn't turn off that feature."

"Would it be illegal for you to look?"

"Not if Renee and I do it together. We'll see how far we can get with her passwords, and then if we need more, we'll have to get to the *good parts*. If it's not illegal for you to break into my room because it's your house, then it shouldn't be illegal for Renee to find her own data. Right?"

"Sounds right to me." Depending on how the "good parts" are accessed, I suppose. Besides, all we really need to know is that it's there so we can show Dylan. That way, maybe he can hold off arresting Renee until the cops figure it all out the proper way to satisfy the rules of evidence. "Let's go find Renee and prove her innocent."

"Okay." Brittany rolls off her bed and then rummages through her backpack, pulling out a laptop I've never seen before. The one I'm familiar with is sitting on the desk in the corner.

"Where did that computer come from?"

Brittany winces. "I'd rather not say. Do you still want my help or not?"

"Yes." I'll cross fingers she didn't steal that laptop and stop asking questions, I guess. Apparently, I'm not cut out for sneaking around electronically any more than I was when Madge and I searched Renee's house. Which reminds me, I need to call Madge and figure out what she knows about Kate.

Brittany and I head downstairs, and she whispers, "It might be better if Gage isn't here while we do this."

"Wait." I stop and hold out my arm to stop her too. "I thought you said it wasn't going to be illegal?"

"It might not have to be. But it could get a little gray, so it'd be better not to have an upholder of the law breathing down our necks, don't you think?"

Brother. "I need to talk to Gage about something anyway, so we'll leave you and Renee alone."

"Thanks, *Jellybean*." Brittany laughs and bounds down the stairs. Like she's excited about what she's about to do. I need to be sure that kid gets into a good college so she'll learn how to use her hacking for something beneficial. And totally legal.

Following behind, I join Brittany, Renee, Cooper, and Gage in the now tidy kitchen. "Gage? Can I speak to you, please? In the living room?" I start down the hall, and he follows.

"What's up, Sawyer?"

I wait until we arrive in the living room, giving myself a moment to kick my nerves to the curb. I need to do this fast. Like ripping off a Band-Aid. I don't want to prolong any pain. "Have a seat. I'd like to talk about you and me."

Gage's brow furrows as he sinks into a red upholstered chair.

I sit on the end of the couch and turn to face him. There's an antique Tiffany lamp on the side table between us, so I push it back a bit. Hopefully, what I have to say won't leave us feeling awkward with each other. I genuinely like Gage and want to be friends.

"Um. I'm not quite sure how to put this—"

Gage holds up a hand to stop me. "I'd like to talk to you too. I know we agreed we'd explore our relationship further, but..." His frown deepens as he struggles for words too.

The worry on my heart lifts when he pauses. Maybe we're both on the same page but just haven't figured that out yet? "Have you developed feelings for Renee?"

"Maybe." Gage blinks in confusion. "I always thought she was way out of my league. That I couldn't be the kind of guy she sees herself with, but after spending more time with her, I'm not so sure. We have much more in common than I realized." He shakes his head as if he still can't wrap it around the idea. "No matter what this is, I'm definitely attracted."

"I noticed. You look at her like I imagine I do my French cookbooks."

"Or Dylan. Your eyes get intense, and you get a little smirk when you speak to him." Gage makes a funny love-struck face. Like the human version of the emoji with heart eyes.

It makes me smile. "Really? I hadn't realized."

He nods. "But you and I connect at a deep level too, right?"

"Yes. So, let's stay friends while we figure Dylan and Renee out." I stick out my hand for a shake. "But if neither of us is married in eight years when I turn forty, you have to marry me. Deal?"

"Deal." He takes my hand and whispers, "But I can't tell Renee how I feel until her legal problems are over. It wouldn't be professional. Can I count on you to keep my secret for now?"

"Absolutely." I lean across the table and kiss his cheek, feeling like a load has been raised from my shoulders. "My lips are sealed until Renee is out of hot water."

He grins and stands. "Sounds like a plan. As was this to get me out of the kitchen while Brittany helps Renee look for her lost data. See you guys tomorrow."

"Yep." Gage is a hard man to fool. "I'll walk you out."

When we get to the front door, Gage stops. "We should still flirt a little, just to keep Renee and Dylan on their toes, right?"

"For sure." I open the front door for him to leave.

Gage slips his hand on my cheek and leans closer. "Maybe I should still kiss you. That way I'll know if I need to move seven and a half years from now rather than be stuck marrying a bad kisser."

He's teasing, but I'm still a bit curious too, so I stand on my tiptoes and lay my lips on his, pleasantly surprised when he deepens our kiss. Taking it to a nice level that makes my toes tingle a bit.

After he leans away, he whispers, "I'll make a note in my phone to book the moving truck in seven years."

"What?" I thought the kiss was a nice one. Not the best ever, but right up there.

"Kidding. You set the bar high. Night, Sawyer."

I playfully punch his arm. "See you tomorrow, brat."

Gage grins as he turns and walks backward down my front lawn. "Operation Find Sawyer A Husband has been in full operation for the last year, you know. Your mom made sure of that, but in the end, she still hoped you'd end up with Dylan. Pretty sure she's smiling right about now." He lifts a hand and then turns to head home.

I let out a heavy sigh and close the door. We'll see how it all turns out.

After flipping the lock, I head for the kitchen to see how Renee and Brittany are doing. Halfway there, my cell rings. I glance at the screen, happy it's Madge. "Hey. So, what's the deal with Kate?"

"I don't know much. Ben, who'd contacted Kate this morning, saw her right after you left and asked how she'd gotten in so quickly from Florida. I couldn't hear all she said. But I did hear Kate say she lied about where she was earlier in case her new phone had been hacked too. Said she left it in San Francisco and drove here so no one could trace her whereabouts. Then Dylan whisked her away to his office and shut the door."

"So was she ever in Florida?"

"That's what I was confused about too. Luckily, Ben filled me in before he went home. He'd sent her an email this morning when the cell number Angelica gave him didn't work. Kate used a new cell she'd bought while visiting family in Florida last week to return his call. She dumped her other cell as soon as she suspected it'd been compromised."

"Where was she during the time of the murder?"

"Ben says Kate was staying with her sister in San Francisco, waiting for Zach to leave Angelica. She'd given up her apartment so she and Zach could move away together. She's been with family since she quit. First her parents in Florida, and then back here to stay with her sister. She was afraid to tell Ben the whole truth this morning because she's convinced someone has hacked her entire life."

"Does she have an alibi for the time of Zach's murder?"

Madge grunts. "Says she was with her sister at the movies. But she definitely lied to Ben this morning, so how can we trust anything she says now?"

"I agree." Especially because Kate apparently told Dylan something about Renee that's going to cause Dylan to arrest her if it checks out in the morning. "How do you get Ben and the other deputies to tell you all this stuff?"

"Men are suckers for baked goods, Sawyer. I promised him I'd bring in my famous brownies tomorrow. Besides, he knows I can snoop in the computer files if I really want to."

"Too bad Dylan doesn't fall for bribes."

Chuckling, Madge says, "We need one person at the station who follows the rules. Gotta run. Talk tomorrow?"

"Yep. Thanks, Madge." I hang up and then join the girls in the kitchen.

After I pet my napping dog, I slip into the nook across from Renee and Brittany. "How's it going?"

Brittany just nods as her fingers fly across the keyboard, but Renee looks up from the screen. "It's going. Did Gage leave? Without saying goodbye?"

"He guessed we were snooping around in your files. Thought it'd be a good time to disappear."

Renee takes a deep drink from her wineglass. "And what was it you two needed to discuss?"

"That Dylan and I need to resolve whatever feelings are still between us. So, for the moment, I'm going to focus on that rather than exploring new relationships."

"Really?" Renee's right brow arches. "How did Gage take it?"

"Fine." I shrug. "We agreed to be friends. So it's all good." I was joking about the marriage thing at forty, so I won't share that part.

Brittany stops typing and glances between us. "Translation. Renee, you can go after Gage if you want." Brittany points her thumb my way. "And this one can stop dancing around her feelings for the sheriff. But more important, someone has been in your accounts big-time, Renee. Someone with major skills. Who didn't want to make it easy to find the data we need to get you off the hook. They changed your cloud passwords."

"But wouldn't I get notification of that?" Renee leans closer to the screen. "I do when my other passwords change."

"You wish." Brittany shakes her head. "They've probably intercepted your emails and are only letting the ones they want to go through. Raphe's dad dealt with a total takeover like this when his software company got hacked. They had to pay the hackers to get the code back. Then they had to move here from the city because Raphe's father lost so much money, they couldn't afford to live downtown anymore."

This sets off an internal alarm. I'd read where large city's computers have been hacked and had to pay ransom to get their information back. Could those same hackers still be blackmailing Raphe's father? Maybe he needs money. "Does Raphe help his dad with the video games?"

"Yeah. He tests how hard the levels are and stuff. Raphe is really good at doing the backgrounds and the sounds. Why?"

That's what I was afraid of. "How can we be sure Raphe isn't involved with this?"

"Because he wouldn't be." Brittany faces Renee. "He likes you. Thinks you're a great boss. No way he'd ever do anything to hurt you."

But what about Raphe's father? I ask Renee, "Has anyone recently helped you with your computers at home or the shop?"

"Yes." Renee winces at her injuries as she slides out of the nook. "Raphe has helped me. With my social media. I pay him to do that stuff at home. He needed the extra money, and I hate that part of running my business."

Brittany frowns. "Does he connect remotely to your system at work?"

"I don't know exactly how he does it. It just gets done." Renee tops off her glass of wine. "He said he needed some software to manage posts I reimbursed him for once. But he only has my passwords to access the social media accounts."

If Renee is like me, the queen of lazy passwords, this could be bad. "Are your social media passwords the same as your others?"

Renee closes her eyes and nods. "Close if not the same. Who can remember all the passwords we use these days?"

"That's what the hackers are counting on," Brittany says as she laces her fingers together and cracks her knuckles. "But I'm good too. I'll find that watch data, if I have to stay up all night long to do it."

Renee slips her arm around Brittany's shoulder. "There'll be free ice cream for life if you can find it. But not a word to Raphe about this, okay? We can't trust anyone else right now. Promise?"

"Yeah. I got your back." Brittany nods as she clicks away at her keyboard again.

The determination on the kid's face helps me believe we can count on Brittany to save the day. But I still have big doubts about Raphe. I think he's involved in this somehow.

Renee tilts her head in a "follow me" gesture and heads out the door, so I trail behind.

Once we're settled on the couches in the living room, she says, "Gage says there's a chance I might be arrested tomorrow. So, I wanted to ask a few favors—"

"Stop. Let's not go there yet. Let's give Brittany a chance to figure things out. We can talk again in the morning."

"Gage said there's too much evidence for Dylan to ignore much longer."

"But it's all circumstantial at this point. And now we have the watch data in your favor. Maybe."

Renee grunts. "Yeah, and an email supposedly from me with the backdoor code to lure Zach into the shop. And let's not forget, the murder weapon belongs to me and has my fingerprints on it. Oh, and here's something new. This afternoon, Dylan showed me an email containing a whole conversation with Zach I don't recognize."

"What was the conversation about?"

"It was a fight where I threatened him."

That's all we need. "Dylan has to see through this. He *knows* you."

"Well, it's pretty hard to argue when Mr. Martinez placed me at the scene near the time of Zach's death. And let's not forget all these scratches and bruises from my fall. It looks so bad, I'd arrest me too in Dylan's shoes."

"The killer couldn't have known you'd fall off your bike. That's just rotten luck."

"But the killer knew a lot. Like where my spare house key is kept. What the codes to my back door at the shop are, but more importantly, that Zach and I had a bad breakup. The texts that he or she sent me had things only Zach and I would know in them."

"How much of your history do your employees know? Other than where your spare key is hidden to water the plants."

"Z didn't know much. She moved here long after Zach left home. Nor Raphe. Annie might remember some stuff from when we were in high school, but whoever the killer is said things that made me believe I was talking to Zach."

"How could someone fake being Zach with intimate details about your relationship without his help? Could he have been working together with someone who turned on him?" I'm thinking about Kate again. What if she and Zach had been up to something together to get money from Angelica? Before he and Kate ran off together? But then, what if Kate got wind of the emails Zach wrote to Renee? And in anger, changed the plan and decided to get rid of Zach and frame Renee?

Maybe Kate then bribed Raphe, who needed extra money, to help her carry out her revenge?

Or could Angelica have done it? Did Angelica know Zach had been cheating with Kate?

The cops always look at the spouse. However, in this case, Angelica never left the bookstore, so she couldn't have physically done it.

People kill for love, hate, and greed. And there's definitely all of that in this scenario.

CHAPTER 11

I'm drying my hair in the bathroom Monday morning, thinking about Angelica, and if she knew about Zach and Kate's alleged affair. I wish I could ask Dylan if Angelica seemed shocked when asked about Kate and her husband, but I'm still banned from speaking to Dylan about the case. Luckily, he seems open to talking about our relationship, so I'll take that for now. Mixing business with pleasure isn't working out so well this week.

When I finish with my hair and makeup, I slip into navy work slacks and a flowy cream blouse. As I head down the hallway, I'm hopeful Brittany will have some good news for us today about Renee's watch information.

I descend the creaky old stairs and poke the swinging door to the kitchen. Brittany, her head on her folded arms in the nook, is softly snoring. Cooper, who's curled up at Brittany's feet, lifts his head and gives me one of his adorable doggy grins while slowly wagging his tail. Almost like he's trying not to wake Brittany.

Onboard with Cooper's efforts, I quietly open the back door for him to go do his business and click it softly shut behind him. When I turn around again, I stop in my tracks at how sweet Brittany looks when asleep. She often seems much older than fifteen, with her black clothing, smirks, and eye rolls. But when she's sleeping, she's just a pretty young girl who wears too much black eyeliner to protect the sweet soul lurking behind her guarded eyes.

Her laptop's screensaver has turned off, so no telling how long she's been asleep.

I cross the kitchen to fill my mug and indulge in one of my life's greatest pleasures—coffee. Closing my eyes, I savor the taste of French vanilla bean dancing across my tongue while filling my veins with the energy I'm afraid I'm going to need today.

Cooper's quiet scratch alerts me that he'd like to come in, so I open the door to find Dylan with Cooper in his arms.

"Morning, Sawyer. Need to see Renee, please."

My coffee turns sour in my gut. "She's still sleeping. Can it wait?" I open the door to let him and my dog pass by.

Dylan sets my dog on all fours. "Afraid not. I need her at the station."

Brittany lifts her head and yawns. "If you're here to arrest her, it'd be a big mistake."

"Why's that?" Dylan's right brow arches.

"Because." Brittany swivels her head back and forth to get the kinks out. "I know it looks like Renee was here in town when Zach was killed. I saw her smartwatch data too. But someone has tampered with it."

Dylan runs a hand down his face. "I thought your online misdeeds were over."

Wait. Dylan knows about Brittany's online scams too? Why am I always the last to know everything? "She wasn't doing anything wrong." I hope. "Renee gave her all the passwords and permission to look at her account."

Brittany nods. "Yeah. The data looks bad, but I found something by analyzing Renee's past rides. It's a ton of information because she rides her bike to work a lot. When I found something odd, I emailed a friend for some help. Then I closed my eyes while I waited for his response, and I guess I fell asleep. Want me to see if he's written back?"

"No." Dylan slides next to Brittany in the booth. "Show me what you found using Renee's passwords."

I pour Dylan some coffee too and slide into the nook across from them. "Who's this friend, Brittany? You promised Renee you wouldn't speak to Raphe about any of this."

Brittany's brows knit. "I have other hacker friends, Sawyer. Geeze." She shakes her head and points to the screen only she and Dylan can see across from me.

Brittany continues, "If Renee is going to ride her bike to work, she usually leaves between eight fifteen, and nine a.m. After the shop opens at ten a.m., she sometimes rides her bike home for lunch and then comes back, or she stays at work all day, locking up at nine p.m."

Dylan nods as he sips coffee. "Sounds right."

"But on Saturday, it looks like she rode her bike to the shop and came home at lunch. And that's the extent of the data. If that were true, her bike would've been at her house when you guys looked for her."

Brittany taps some keys. "I wrote a quick program that put all the times and dates of her rides into a spreadsheet. Look at this. Because the time stamp records tenths of seconds too, I couldn't find any two days when Renee left her house and arrived home at exactly at the same time. Except for these. The day of the murder and another one."

Dylan leans closer to the screen. "Last May."

"That's right." A slow grin forms on Brittany's face as she taps more keys. "But the time isn't the only thing the watch records if you click deeper. And this is where the hacker screwed up. The temperature, heart rate, elevation change, and a bunch of other things are also recorded for people serious about biking or running, but it's stored in a different place. Someone copied old data and replaced the real data."

"The temperatures in August would have been warmer than the temperatures last May." Intensity fills Dylan's gaze as he faces Brittany. "All we have to do is verify weather condition differences on those two days, right? To prove that someone changed the data."

"Exactly!" Brittany raises her hand for a high five.

Dylan's hands remained wrapped around his mug. "This

might have gotten Renee off, but now, how do I know you didn't hack into the database and replace the real data to make all this unreliable?"

Brittany's hand quickly drops. "Because I didn't."

"For all we know, this could also be a database glitch. Without the real data to match Renee's story, you stayed up all night for nothing." Dylan takes his mug to the dishwasher and drops it inside. "This wasn't a smart idea, ladies. Now the lab will see a strange computer logged onto the cloud last night using Renee's password. Not that she doesn't have a right to look at her own information, but it could create more doubt. Especially because the computer Brittany used probably has an IP address that has visited a few sites it shouldn't. Am I right, Brittany?"

Brittany's eyes narrow. "Not if I covered my tracks properly, *Sheriff*. But using your logic, there should also be another IP address not belonging to Renee or me that logged into Renee's account sometime since May. Maybe your cop friends should start looking there. If they need help figuring out who the IP address belongs to, let me know. I'm going to tell Renee what I found. At least *she'll* thank me." Brittany stands and smacks the swinging door as hard as she can before she passes through it.

After she's gone, I whisper, "She was just trying to help. And I doubt she left any trace that she'd been in Renee's account. She's evidently very good."

"That's what I've heard." Dylan huffs out a breath as he sinks into the nook again. "But if she isn't as good as she claims, I'll have one more hurdle to clear that I don't need right now."

I reach out and weave my fingers through his. "On the other hand, she saved you guys a ton of work. And I'd guess if she knows how to cover her IP address, then she can probably also help you figure out how to trace the blackmailer's identity too. You heard her, she has more than one hacker friend." I smile and give his hand a squeeze. "Can you deputize a kid? She might come in handy."

Unamused, he says, "No. Now can you go get Renee, please?"

My blood runs cold. "You can't arrest Renee after what Brittany showed you. At least wait until the lab catches up with what Brittany found. Please?"

"I have to follow procedures."

"I understand. But can't you make an exception just this once? For me?" This is where that rock-and-a-hard-place problem Gage warned me about rears its ugly head.

I'm holding my breath, waiting for his response. Dylan is rubbing the back of his neck like he does when he's frustrated when Brittany busts through the door again.

She skids to a stop and declares, "Renee's gone. And I'm not sure her bed has been slept in."

Dylan takes off with a curse toward the stairs. "This is what I get for making exceptions, Sawyer. Renee should have been safely in custody yesterday, but I held off because of the watch."

I'm having a hard time drawing in air.

What if Renee ran? But if she's innocent, why do that?

I RUN AFTER DYLAN UPSTAIRS. I take the bathroom and Dylan takes the bedroom Renee is staying in. But Renee isn't anywhere to be found. Her bed is made and her closet empty, but then it always was. She'd stopped by her house yesterday with Gage to change before she went into the station.

Dylan says, "Maybe she went home for more clothes?"

"Could be." Or maybe she didn't want to be arrested, so she left town. Better to keep that thought to myself, though. "I doubt she'd go for a run. She's still limping from her bike injuries."

Dylan stops searching through drawers and says, "Maybe she's at her spot. I'm sure Gage told her I'd most likely have to take her into custody today."

Her spot. High on the cliffs overlooking the ocean, she always went to as a kid when her parents were fighting again or she was upset about something. Why didn't I think of that? "I'll go look. Can you at least ask the lab people to check the watch data starting last May? Please? In the meantime, I promise I'll bring Renee to you at the station as soon as I find her."

Dylan pulls his phone from his pocket and taps out a message. "I updated the lab and asked for a rush. That's the best I can do. Go open your shop, and I'll find Renee."

"But—"

Dylan cuts me off. "Don't make this harder than it already is. I'll talk to you later." He turns to leave.

I follow him down the stairs and ask, "What about Kate? Why isn't she locked up too?"

Dylan hits the bottom step and heads for the front door. "She's being kept somewhere safe. Call me if you hear from Renee."

Somewhere safe? In Sunset Cove? Nowhere is safe from gossip in this town. Everyone will know where she's staying within an hour. Unless... Before he can make it to the door, I say, "Stop right there, Dylan Cooper."

He turns around. "I'm in a hurry, Sawyer."

I catch up to him in the hall and cross my arms, whispering so Brittany won't hear in the kitchen. "Since when is it the sheriff's job to keep beautiful suspects in his guest room? Assuming that's the bed she slept in."

Dylan runs a hand down his face. "Since when do you care who spends the night at my house? Not that I'm saying she did."

Oh, she did all right. Dylan's red cheeks prove it.

I tamp down the pangs of jealousy I have no right to have. We haven't been together for years. "I'm just saying it's not fair to arrest Renee and then let Kate run free. Kate has a motive, and she was nearby during the murder. She'd been having an affair with Zach, and she has a computer science degree. Those things are just as incriminating as what you have against Renee. And yet, you're going to make breakfast and bat your eyelashes at Kate while throwing Renee in jail.

Renee, who you've know all your life, I might add!" So much for staying calm.

Dylan leans down. "I have a plan to catch the killer. That includes doing all I can to keep everyone, including Renee, safe. Even if that means arresting her. And if you keep up your sleuthing, you might find yourself sharing a bunk in a cell with your best pal for the same reason. *Capisce?*"

Capisce? What is he, the Godfather now?

Dylan leans closer, "But don't worry. Kate's eggs don't hold a candle to yours."

"Very funny." I poke his big shoulder. "Go find Renee before I give you a reason to arrest me."

Ignoring my false threat, he says, "Can I trust you to go open your store and stay out of trouble today? Please?"

"Of course. Unless trouble finds me *first*. Be safe." I wrap my arms around his massive shoulders and give him a quick hug. "If Renee isn't at her spot, will you call me?"

"I'll call you either way." Dylan opens the front door but stops halfway out. "Really, Sawyer. Go to work and let me do my job. Okay?"

"That's the plan." Before Dylan hits the sidewalk, I call out, "Hey, Sheriff?"

"What?" He stops and raises his brows.

"In the future, I officially care who spends the night at your house."

Dylan's face lights with one of his cute grins. "Understood." He turns and heads toward the cliffs and Renee's spot.

I smile and head back inside before reality catches up with me again. Dylan made it sound like Renee could be in some sort of danger. All the more reason to keep helping her, albeit from my store as I promised.

Perhaps an emergency meeting of the book club is in order.

I'M AT THE BOOKSTORE, pacing and worrying about Renee, when my phone rings.

It's Dylan. "Hi. Did you find Renee?"

"She was at her spot."

Relief washes over me. "Good. Will you have to keep her after you question her?"

"Can't discuss that with you," he says with a tired sigh.

"It'll get crowded at your house with Kate there too." If it were anyone other than Renee, I might be worried about all these women in Dylan's house.

"I never confirmed Kate's location, but it's important we don't talk about where Kate or Renee are for now. Okay?"

"Okay. Fine. But—"

He interrupts, "No more questions. Your quota is used up for the day. I'll call you later if I can. Bye."

"Bye." I hang up and let out a long breath. It's frustrating to be unable to help. Maybe the book club will come up with a plan. And speaking of them, I need to figure out what to serve at our emergency meeting.

I'll look at it as an opportunity to try out a new sandwich for my menu because I'm a believer in multitasking.

Brittany wants a California burrito with carne asada, pico, guacamole, and cheese but that's a staple offered everywhere around here. My spicy fish tacos might be a good alternative. Or a simple Caprese sandwich. Who doesn't like a nice roll with mozzarella, onion, tomatoes, and basil all covered with a good balsamic vinegar? But this is California, home of the avocado, so I should keep it simple yet trendy—avocado toast with fresh fruit on the side.

In the little kitchenette at my bookshop, I mash the fresh avocados with lemon juice and then lift my hand high above the bowl to add salt and pepper. When it's well blended, I spread the mixture over a thick piece of toasted sourdough bread baked fresh daily in San Francisco, drizzle my imported olive oil over the top, and lightly dust it all with red pepper and delicate sea salt flakes. I debate adding an over-easy egg but decide against it. Mostly because I don't do my best egg work on hot plates. My mom left me a commercial-grade stovetop for that at home that I will always be grateful for.

Brittany helps me plate the fruit salad and sets out the pitchers of iced tea. With my bribe in place—or should I call it an enticement to interrupt their workdays to help Renee—we're ready for the meeting to begin.

The bell above the front door tinkles, announcing the arrival of either a rare customer or a book club member.

Glancing over my shoulder, I smile. "Hi, Admiral. Right on time."

He nods his white-haired head. "Wouldn't miss this for the world, Sailor." He pulls out a chair at one of the little round bistro tables and sits with a thump. "Your mother would be so proud of you. She always knew you had it in you."

Brittany sets a glass of iced tea in front of our guest. "Always had what in her, Admiral?"

He takes a long drink, sets his glass down, and says, "I don't recall. But Sailor has it. That's for sure!"

Brittany stifles a grin as she fills the other glasses with tea.

Next, Madge flies through the door with her knitting bag in her hand. "Only have a half hour for lunch today. On account of the murder investigation and all." She sits and pulls out her metal needles. "Do you have a warm sweater for winter, Sawyer? It'll get chilly soon."

It's only August. And the last thing I want is to have to wear one of Madge's goofy Christmas sweaters to be polite. "I used to live in Chicago, remember? Where we had real winters. I think I can handle the brutal Sunset Cove midfifties."

Madge shrugs. "The breeze off the ocean can make it feel cooler. Never hurts to spread a little Christmas cheer either. Not that big-city people would understand the sense of community we have here. So, if you're all set..."

"I really am, thanks." Pangs of guilt poking me in the

chest make me add, "But one of your amazing designs to spread holiday cheer would be greatly appreciated." My fingers are crossed behind my back to protect me from the bolts of lightning waiting to strike me dead.

"Great! I'll get right on it." Madge smiles as she digs into the sandwich Brittany placed in front of her.

When the bell rings again, I see the gang's all here. Julie, the pretty blonde who works at the grocery store, and the new guy Nick, who's tall, thin, and wears a Star Trek T-shirt, join us.

We used to have two more members, Wade and Chad, but Wade killed Chad, so that put a big dent in our membership numbers. Wade, who's currently in prison, asked if he could video-chat with us each week from his cell, but I nixed that idea. Mostly because he tried to kill me too. I'm usually a fairly forgiving person, but I draw the line at attempted murder.

Nick pulls out a chair for Julie and sits beside her. He glances my way and pokes a finger at the bridge of his black glasses. "Hi, Sawyer. The mayor says not to come back without you. He wants to speak to you before the merchants' meeting this afternoon."

I'd almost forgotten about that meeting. Almost. And I don't want to go to my uncle's office, but I really don't want Nick to suffer the wrath of my uncle if I skip it. "Okay. Let's get started while everyone eats."

Brittany and I join the others and do a full recap of the facts of Renee's case we know so far. After I'm done, I take a big bite of my toast and withhold a moan. It's darn good if I do say so myself. "Any ideas on how to proceed from here?"

Nick, late twenties, computer expert, brown haired, and who must've had braces as a kid because his teeth are weirdly perfectly straight, says, "They always return to the scene of the crime, right? It's like serial killer 101. They like, have to. It's in their DNA."

Julie raises her hand because she's the polite type. "But only if it's a man. I think. Women don't do that, do they?"

Nick shrugs because his mouth is full.

The Admiral wipes his hands on his napkin and says, "Women serial killers are rare. But in this case, we're talking about a single homicide. As far as we know."

Madge, her plate clean and her needles busy clicking away, adds, "Yes. But the exception is crimes of passion. With women, I mean. Zach was cheating, so there's the passion aspect. But would a woman really be strong enough to hit Zach in the back of the head and kill him? Zach was tall, let's not forget."

"Sledgehammers make up for lack of muscle," Nick says. "But Renee is tall too, right?"

"Yes, but it wasn't a very big sledgehammer. Not much bigger than a regular hammer except for the end." Madge frowns. "And we haven't heard if the blow to the head killed Zach or if hitting his noggin on the corner of the table did him in."

"Doesn't matter," Brittany finally chimes in. "I say we look at the hackers. Who could've hired muscle for the kill."

"And I say we need to see who shows up at the funeral tomorrow." The Admiral stands and takes his plate to the sink. "Isn't that another form of returning to the crime scene? Wouldn't the killer get a twisted rush out of watching everyone grieve and wonder who among them might have done it?"

Nick chuckles. "That's the way it worked in old movies from like ten years ago. But it's not a bad idea. I could install a camera in the alley behind Renee's shop too in case the killer comes back. And we could film at the funeral parlor during the service."

I stand to gather dirty dishes. "We'd have to have permission from the funeral parlor to film, wouldn't we?"

Nick glances at Brittany, and they share a "poor uninformed people look." He says, "Brittany can use her cell phone. No one will pay any attention to a bored kid on her cell phone wearing earbuds. She'll mingle and record video and sound. We aren't looking for Hollywood quality here. Want me to stick a camera in the alley behind Renee's shop or not?"

I nod. "She said she regretted not adding cameras back there, so Renee won't mind." I turn and face Brittany. "Do you want to do this?"

"Absolutely. Renee fed me when I was starving. I owe her." Brittany smirks. "And technically, I'm the perfect person for the recording job because I'm a minor. How much trouble can I get into for being a mischievous kid? If caught,

I'll just tell Dylan I'm thinking of going into filmmaking, so this was a practice run."

While everyone else nods in agreement and Brittany and Nick high five, I still have doubts. It's a big job for a kid. And if caught, could it be dangerous for Brittany? "Nope. I'll do the recording. I can't risk Brittany getting noticed by the killer."

All heads turn my way. Nick finally says, "No offense, Sawyer, but you're way too old to pull this off. Brittany is the only one here who'll blend. And we don't have time to install real equipment that could be spotted by the killer if he or she shows up. The funeral is at ten tomorrow morning."

Since when is thirty-two old?

We all want Renee to be freed and the real killer exposed, but at what cost? The killer isn't stupid. He or she did a fantastic job of making Renee look guilty. Nick's right. I *would* look suspicious whereas Brittany wouldn't. "Fine. But we all have to work together to keep eyes on Brittany at all times. I'll try to stick by her side, but if I have to leave, I need one of you to take my place. And, we're all going to be armed."

Madge grins. "I'll have my gun in my purse, so count me in."

"I wasn't talking about guns." I walk behind the counter and grab the Taser flashlights I started stocking after our last scare with Wade. They were cheaper to buy in bulk. And if I purchased them as inventory, the store/trust paid for them. "These will be in backpacks or purses at all times. Charge them up tonight." I hand them out to everyone. "So, are we all in?"

Smiles abound as everyone nods and grabs their Tasers, that double as a nice flashlight in case of a power outage.

I force a smile too. "See you all tomorrow at the funeral, then."

Brittany scoots beside me as we watch everyone file out of the store. When they're all gone, she says, "Not that I'm having any second thoughts, but Dylan is going to kill you if he finds out what we're up to."

I let out a long sigh. "I know. But hopefully we'll expose the killer, and then he'll cut me some slack. Or I'll just become a recluse nun."

Brittany snorts in response as Nick comes rushing back in the door. "I almost forgot. I'm supposed to deliver you to the mayor now. Something about your trust?"

Great.

I'd rather have a root canal.

CHAPTER 12

I'm dreading the meeting that I've been summoned to. I've successfully avoided my Uncle Frank since the last financial meeting where we went over the bookstore's earnings reports. By adding an online store, Brittany and I have managed to make a slight profit, but it's not much to be proud of. As my uncle so helpfully pointed out.

Nick and I walk in silence side by side down the tiled hall to the mayor's office in the municipal building as I go over all the highlights of the trust. He's been asking for this meeting for a few weeks, so I've tried to read all the boring legalese. I don't want to appear unprepared for this meeting.

The only good thing about the inherited trust my grand-parents set up for my mom and uncle is it was designed to ensure my mom always had a roof over her head and food on the table. Technically, my uncle can't shut down the store. Just wait me out until I get so tired of being poor that I leave and find a real job. Then all the assets would revert to him and he can do whatever he wants with them. Unlike me. I can't sell anything. Only maintain the properties I've inherited. I'm only wealthy on paper. The trust has millions to maintain its assets, but my bank account currently has a whopping five hundred dollars in it.

My grandparents feared my mom's free-spirited and kind heart would compel her to donate all the wealth they left to her to a homeless shelter or some such. But she was shrewd enough to help me find a way to work around the silly trust restrictions after she died by leaving me her secret stash of expensive wine she'd inherited from a fellow book lover.

My uncle thinks I'm using the trust's money to build out the space next to my bookstore for a wealthy celebrity chef from San Francisco who has sworn his legal representative, Gage, to secrecy. The town council made that bad assumption all on their own. And maybe with a little help from Gage, but it's all in the public record. No one lied to them. Gage presented the business plan to the council as a wealthy chef who wants to keep his/her identity private until the grand opening.

My uncle is going to blow an artery when he figures out that I'm the chef—wealthy only on paper, but still, I'm going to savor the moment. For my mom's and sister's sakes too.

Nick opens the outer door to the mayor's office for me. "Good luck. I hear he's in a mood today."

"Worse than his normal sour disposition?" I ask.

"Yep. See ya tomorrow. I'll install the camera behind Renee's shop after work tonight." He turns to leave.

"Thanks, Nick." I throw my shoulders back and prepare to meet the lion in his den.

While drawing a deep breath, I step inside and make my way to the receptionist's desk. A woman busy typing on her keyboard is in her early thirties with jet-black hair, and looks familiar, but I'm not able to come up with her name. "Hi. Is my uncle in? He's expecting me."

The woman stops her tapping, and her dark eyes focus intently on mine. "He's at the golf course for a meeting with his staff. He said to have you wait." Her eyes do an up and down over my body. "You don't remember me, do you?"

My mind races as a weird dread fills my stomach. I don't think I liked her back in the day, but I can't put my finger on why. "No. I'm so sorry. I'm the worst with names, though."

"How about a hint?" A slow, almost evil grin spreads across her face. "I was the one kid less popular than you in school. That is until you started dating the golden boy, and all the kids tolerated you because of him."

Dylan *was* popular. High school quarterback and all-around nice guy. I was the smart nerd who wore hand-me-downs and ate instant oatmeal and leftover croissants from the bookstore for lunch because that was all we could afford most of the time.

I never knew what Dylan saw in me but was glad for whatever it was. He changed my life for the better. Helped me have the confidence to go away to school and to follow my dreams. I wish he would've let me help him after his mom died and his dad ran off with... That's who the receptionist is. The daughter of the woman Dylan's father ran off with.

Beth Dugan. Kids used to call her the teenaged witch because she had voodoo dolls and weird bags of herbs she wore around her neck to ward off evil spirits. She'd poke needles into Renee and Dylan dolls in front of me in homeroom and whisper how I didn't deserve them to be my friends.

Beth's eyes narrow in challenge. "You just figured it out, didn't you?"

Did the horrified look on my face give me away?

It's an odd day when I'd rather spend time with my mean uncle than someone like Beth. Could things get more awkward? "Beth. It's nice to see you again."

She snorts. "Doubt it. But I've been meaning to talk to Dylan about something. Maybe you could give him a message from me?"

My palms are sweating. I hope this doesn't have to do with any more needles and dolls. "Sure. What's up?"

She stands to her full six-foot height and circles her desk to look down at all five and a half feet of me.

Beth says, "I'm concerned about Dylan's father. I've been getting disturbing vibes from my water readings."

I don't even want to know what water readings are. In

the movies, people see visions in pools of liquid. "What kind of vibes?"

She places her hand on my left shoulder. "Around here. Like something's wrong with his heart. And he wants to tell Dylan something that's been burdening him."

A slow-building heat forms under her hand. It's freaking me out, so I take a step back. "Have you told your mom?"

Beth smiles as if she's enjoying how spooked I am. "Of course. But she says Walt is too stubborn to go to the doctor. Maybe Dylan could convince him otherwise."

If Beth were really psychic or whatever, she'd know speaking to Dylan won't help. As far as I know, Dylan hasn't spoken to his dad since his mother's funeral when we were seniors in high school. "I'll be sure to pass your concerns on to Dylan. Why don't you ask the mayor to stop by my store on his way back?" I head toward the door, wanting out as fast as I can.

"No!" Beth jogs to the door, trapping me inside. "Frank said to have you wait in his office. So, go. Wait." She frowns and folds her long arms—tattooed with odd celestial symbols—leaving no room to argue.

"Fine." Happy to be anywhere but in Beth's creepy presence, I practically run into the connecting office and close the heavy door behind me.

I've never been alone in my uncle's office before. He usually seeks me out in my bookstore to try to intimidate me, or when we meet in the accountant's office.

The walls are covered with pictures of my hulking uncle

at his new golf course just outside town. He's posing with all sorts of local businesspeople and even a few celebrities from San Francisco. He looms over everyone with his bald head and muscle-bound body. I always think of him as a mean version of Mr. Clean from TV ads.

There's only one older picture of my uncle with his family. It includes my quiet aunt, who has never stood up to him, and my two older male cousins who moved away from Sunset Cove as fast as they could after college—more likely it was their dad they were trying to escape.

There's a massive desk scattered with stacks of papers and bookshelves overflowing with mismatched books and golf trophies. In the corner of the office, my uncle has set up a mini putting course with those electronic machines that spit the ball out if you make it in. Looks like fun while I wait, so I lean down and pick up one of the golf balls scattered about the mini course. It's the same brand of ball that broke my store's window a few weeks ago. The partially obscured message on that ball warned me to go back home. I suspected it was my uncle trying to scare me, but Madge got a hold of his handwriting, and the sample didn't match. No matter who threw it, I won't be intimidated by a little golf ball through my window.

I drop the ball to the carpet and tap it with the putter into the first hole. The ball is ejected with a satisfying pop, so I aim for the second hole and then the third. Just as the ball is about to hit the little ramp, the door swings open and Beth walks in.

"Frank just called. He's on the way. And he said to stop playing with his stuff."

"How would he even... Never mind." I lay down the putter. She's probably just messing with me. Or she heard the machine spit the balls out. "Thanks for letting me know." I drop into the leather chair in front of my uncle's desk to wait.

Beth stands in the doorway, studying me for a few moments before she finally says, "You don't believe in my powers, but I saw a vision of who hit the ball through your store's window. When you're ready to stop being a skeptic, I'll tell you who did it." The door snaps shut behind her.

Oh, please. She's obviously loyal to my uncle. He probably told her to hire a tourist kid to throw the ball through my window and then disappear to wherever he came from. That's how she'd know who did it. Or maybe she did it!

I'm a logical person who believes there's a reasonable answer for everything. One just has to look to find it. But still, a cold shiver slips up my spine.

The next time the door opens, my uncle strides in. "Sawyer. Thanks for coming. I have a proposition you'll want to consider."

My guard flies up to DEFCON 1. "Really? What's that?"

My uncle slithers into his big leather chair like the snake he is. "I need to know who the celebrity chef is going to be for the new restaurant. Tell me that, and I'll tell the merchants to leave you alone about your bookstore being out of compliance."

"If I can't talk the committee into letting me keep my storefront and signs the way they are, I'll have the trust pay for the renovations. So if that's all, I have to run."

"Hold on." My uncle holds up his beefy hand. "It's not that simple. If you don't comply with the new rules just passed by the town council, we can legally shut down your bookstore."

"New rules just passed? Were these rules 'just passed' since I moved home?"

"As a matter of fact, yes." My uncle grins and leans back in his chair. "Your bookstore is an eyesore that's out of compliance. You'll have to tear down your façade and make the repairs within thirty days, or we'll shut you down."

He's worse than a snake. He's pond scum. "But if I tell you who the chef is, you'll break your own new rules?"

"The mayor has the power to grant a grandfather clause, if deemed necessary. And by the way, I've filed to freeze the funds in the trust until we get a ruling on the legality of your mother adopting and adding Brittany to the family without my knowledge. So there won't be any money for your restaurant space or the repairs to your bookstore unless you play nice with me."

This could ruin all my plans. I don't want to have to take a chef's job in San Francisco to support me and Brittany. The daily commute would kill me. Besides, I've dreamed of having my own restaurant for years. I need to think of something. Fast.

An excuse to hold my uncle off pops into my head. "I'd have to talk to Gage. About confidentiality papers I signed." I

A NOVEL WAY TO DIE

actually did sign a confidentiality agreement with Gage that he, thankfully, insisted on. But that was about him keeping *my* identity a secret.

My uncle shrugs. "I won't tell anyone else."

"That's not the way it works. I could be sued for breach of contract."

"No one would ever know you told me. Besides, I've asked around, and that wine your mom left you isn't enough. You need the trust's money to build out the space for your new tenant. Not to mention keeping that money pit of a house your mom left you from falling down."

What am I going to do?

I can repair the front of my bookstore by selling some wine, but he's right, I can't build out a whole restaurant space with that wine money, even if I sell all of it. I need the trust money for that. I planned to rent the space and all the equipment inside to the new restaurant that I'll own outright to make my plan work.

My uncle circles the desk and sits on the edge, looming over me. "Or you and I can make a deal right now. A one-time offer that expires in exactly ten minutes. I'll give you two million bucks to take that degenerate child and leave town. That's more money than you'll ever see from the trust the way it stands. The most you can ever hope for is rent money from that new chef. Assuming the restaurant makes it. Most don't, according to my research. Then you and that kid will be right back in the poor house again."

"The tourist trade from San Francisco alone can keep

the restaurant in the black. I've done my research too. And Brittany isn't a degenerate. She's a good kid." Man, I'm in a tight spot. Can my uncle legally freeze the trust fund? "I need to talk to Gage. But you can tell your corrupt little merchants' coven that I'll start on the repairs to my book-store right away. I have to run." I'll ask Annie's husband to start on my store before my house, especially because now there might not be money to fix that either for a while. My uncle must stay up nights dreaming up ways to run me out of town.

"You still have seven minutes to do yourself the biggest favor of your life. It's two million bucks, Sawyer. More money than you'll ever see the rest of your life. Tick-tock."

That *is* a lot of money. And I never planned to live in Sunset Cove. I was happy in Chicago.

Wasn't I?

I ponder and chew my thumbnail as my uncle gloats over his watch.

He says, "It's an all-cash deal. If your mom did something illegal by adding Brittany, the whole trust might be mine anyway. I'm only being generous because you're family. Six minutes and counting."

My mom wanted me to stay, raise Brittany, and open the restaurant of my dreams. But two million dollars isn't anything to pass up lightly. It could be a great new start for us. And I doubt my mom checked with a lawyer about the trust before she adopted Brittany. She couldn't stand the lawyers who run our trust. "You'd transfer the cash from the trust directly to my account?" I know there's millions in various accounts. I've seen the bank statements.

"Absolutely." A slow, triumphant grin crosses my uncle's face. "It can be done within ten days. I'm sure you saw the rules for distribution in the trust. You only have four minutes left to decide."

I *have* read the trust. It's how I figured out how to outsmart it with my restaurant. And I also know that my uncle stands to make ten times what he's offering me if I throw in the towel and he gets all my mom's properties. He'd sell them to investors just dying to expand our little quiet hamlet.

If I can pull off my restaurant, who knows how many of my other properties I can improve and rent out as well? My uncle kept my mom under his big fat thumb because she was too nice to argue with him. But I'm not that nice. He mistreated my mom, my sister, and me all our lives. Allowed us to live just above the poverty line while he and his family prospered on my grandparents' wealth.

There wasn't a provision about adopting kids that I saw in the trust paperwork. There could be some loopholes I missed…but I'm willing to take the risk.

Even if I fail, I won't be any worse off than I was a year ago. Besides, Dylan loves it here and would never leave. I have a second chance to see where that might go. Being happy was all my mom wanted for me and Megan. Not to be rich. I'll just take my chances that I can one day beat my uncle at his own game. For my mom's sake if nothing else.

"Make it twenty million, closer to what my share is worth, and we have a deal. I'll give you thirty seconds to decide."

"Don't be ridiculous." My uncle slowly shakes his head. "You're just as dense as your mother was. She turned down my generous offer too. The clock starts now on your thirty days to renovate your bookstore. Good luck hiring any help. As of this afternoon, I've got all the contractors in a fifty-mile radius tied up with my new golf course expansion. To be certain you fail."

I stand and grab my purse. "Mom always said karma will bite you in your greedy butt one day. And I'm going to do my best to prove her right."

My uncle shakes his head. "I'll be laughing all the way to the bank while you try. Shut the door on your way out."

Not only did I shut his door, I slammed it for good measure.

STILL FUMING, I stop in the corridor outside my uncle's office and dial Charlie's number. I'm hoping Annie's husband can start on my storefront Wednesday morning instead of my house. When I get their voicemail, I leave a message and hang up. I'll have to find the specs for the façade I got at the last merchants' meeting. I think I tossed it in a drawer under the cash register, but I'll have to hunt it down tonight.

Madge sticks her head out down the hall and calls out,

"Sawyer. Thank goodness. Brittany told me you were here meeting with your uncle. Come here. Quick. It's Dylan."

Dylan? My heart pounds as I race toward the station.

I skid to a stop and ask, "What's wrong?"

Madge grabs my arm and tugs me inside. "I don't know. His brother called. After Dylan hung up, he slammed his office door closed, and it sounds like he's kicking furniture in there. When I knocked to check on him, he growled at me to go away."

I jog to Dylan's closed office door and knock. "Dylan? Can I come in?"

His voice bellows, "Not now, Sawyer. I'll call you later."

I glance at Madge and whisper, "Has he ever acted like this before?"

She shakes her head. "Something your brother-in-law said really upset him."

I make an executive decision and open the door, quickly closing it behind me. "If this is about the kids or my sister, I need to know too."

Dylan, who's sitting at his desk with his head in his hands moans, "They're all fine. It's my father. Please just go and let me deal with this."

His father? Could Beth's woo-woo business have been right? My knees grow weak before I pull myself together. "I can't leave you like this." I circle around Dylan's desk and wrap an arm around his shoulders. "What happened?"

"Please. Just stop!"

My head jerks back at the bite in his tone. "Stop what?"

171

"I understand you grew up having to solve all your parents' problems, and you still feel compelled to fix everything in everyone's life, but this is one problem you can't solve, Sawyer! I asked you not to bother me, but as usual, you never listen. Please leave me alone."

The anger in his tone is like none I've ever heard from him. And it isn't the first time I've been told I have an annoying habit of trying to fix everything. But it's because I care. Especially about him.

I swallow the hurt that's rising in my throat, threatening to make me cry, and croak out, "I'm sorry I bothered you." I give his shoulders a quick squeeze and then head slowly for the door.

Just as I turn the knob to leave, Dylan lets out a long resigned sigh. "Wait. Don't go."

Relief fills me that he's not throwing me out of his life— along with his office—as I sit in one of the guest chairs in front of his desk. I want to ask a million questions, but just this once, maybe I'll bite my tongue.

Dylan scrubs his hands down his face. "There was a car accident. My father is in the hospital. Lance thinks I should go to San Diego to see my dad in case he doesn't make it. But I can't. I have a murderer on the loose."

I'm sorry for the accident but glad to know it wasn't a heart attack like Beth predicted a few minutes ago. That would've been too freaky for my mind to wrap around. "Madge and the deputies can hold the fort for a day. You could catch a flight this afternoon and be back tomorrow afternoon." I slide my hand over his. "My mom held on too long just to be sure I knew she loved me. Don't let your dad go without patching things up. He loves you too."

Dylan's brow furrows. "He never loved anyone but himself. You don't know the whole story. I'm staying here. End of discussion."

"Okay." In other words, butt out. "I'm sorry about your dad. I'll see you later." I start for the door again but stop. How wouldn't I know all the details about his father? Dylan and I were inseparable in high school before his father left. "Does Lance know about whatever's bothering you about your dad?"

"No." Dylan's eyes start to mist before he quickly blinks the moisture away. "He loves Dad, and I don't want to be the one to change that. I'll let Lance believe our dad was the good guy he wanted everyone to think he was."

"Seems to me the secret you've been carrying has caused you a lot more distress than it has your father." Lance and Megan have visited Dylan's dad at his beach house in San Diego many times. He apparently got rich selling his medical practice and has lived well ever since. "Maybe it's time to forgive him for whatever he did and let things go."

Dylan's jaw clenches. "I'll never forgive him."

"Never is a long time." I open the door to leave. It takes all my willpower to move my feet forward when all I want to do is give Dylan a hug. But he made it clear he doesn't want any help or sympathy from me.

Dylan quietly adds, "What my father did was unforgivable. And by keeping his secret, I'm just as guilty."

Okay. Maybe Dylan's not done after all.

I shut the door and sit quietly in the chair again.

Dylan stands and paces back and forth, like he's having some sort of internal debate with himself. After a few moments he says, "Fine. I'll tell you. But you have to promise you won't tell anyone else. Especially your sister."

"Okay. But you don't have to tell me if you'd rather not. I'll still be here for you either way."

Dylan sits beside me in the other guest chair and takes my hand. "My dad wrote false prescriptions to get rich. Then, after getting my mom hooked on drugs, he left her and us behind. After he'd left, my mom feared her addiction would come to light. She had nowhere to get the drugs he'd supplied her. This town is too small to hide something like that."

"I'm so sorry." I give his hand a squeeze. "I had no idea."

He nods. "She was distraught about my father leaving and her inability to quit the drugs, so she drove off the cliff and killed herself to save Lance and me the shame of having a junkie mother."

All the air whooshes from my lungs. We all thought her death was an accident. How could that have been going on without me noticing? Not that we spent much time at his house. We usually spent time at mine, because my mom was so lenient. Now I can see why Dylan never wanted to be home. "How did you find this out?"

"I overheard my parents fighting one night after Lance left for college. She begged my father to help her get off the drugs. He told her it was her problem. She threatened to kill herself, and he told her to go ahead. It'd be cheaper for him in the divorce if she did."

I want to be sick. "And you kept that in all these years?"

"I had no choice. When I didn't go to the cops right away, I was just as guilty." Dylan shakes his head in disgust. "I bet the stress from keeping his secret is what caused my father to have a heart attack on the freeway."

A heart attack? So, Beth's vision was right? I'll have to think about that later, though, because for now, I'm more worried about Dylan. "You were a kid mourning your mom. Surely the court would see it that way. As opposed to you covering for your dad."

"After my mom died, I confronted him. My dad begged me not to tell about his fake prescriptions and ruin his life. And I stupidly agreed. Because I delivered most of those drugs to people for him."

That's how Dylan made money after school. Running errands for his dad. "But you didn't know. You couldn't have known, Dylan."

"Looking back, I should have known. I was so focused on the money, I never questioned things. And later, when I asked him to confess because the guilt was eating me alive, he reminded me I was eighteen and an adult when I agreed to protect him. So, I'd go to jail too. It's why I joined the military. I hoped I'd be killed doing the right thing rather than stay here doing something wrong."

I blink in shock while I absorb his words. "And when you didn't die, you decided to come back here and uphold the law? To make up for a mistake you made as a kid in high school, manipulated by your father? Trying to hold on to the only other parent you had?"

Dylan closes his eyes. "It's why I didn't want to get married and saddle you with my burdens. I was afraid I'd go to jail if the secret came out." He opens his eyes and stares into mine. "I'd hoped you'd find a nice guy and live the life you deserve, Sawyer."

I whisper, "Would you go to jail if you confessed now?" I'm holding my breath. Dreading the answer.

Finally, he says, "No. The statute of limitations has passed. But can you understand why I want nothing to do with my father?"

"I do. But..." I don't want to put any stock in Beth's weird powers, but I feel like I need to share what she told me. "Beth predicted your dad's heart attack just a few minutes ago in the mayor's office. She also said your dad wants to tell you something that's been burdening him. That could've all come from your stepmother and not Beth's so-called powers, but maybe you owe it to yourself to talk to your dad. Maybe he'll take the responsibility for his actions and let you off the guilt train for good."

Dylan releases my hand and sits behind his desk again.

"Lance said Dad really wants to tell me something. But what difference will it make?"

"How do you know until you hear what he has to say? If it's not an apology, tell him you want one. You deserve that, Dylan."

"Yeah." He rubs the back of neck as he considers. "I guess I do."

"I'll book your flights and then text you with the details. Go home, pack, and I'll drive you to the airport. But then no matter what happens, you need to forgive yourself."

"There you go again. Fixing things." A slow smile crosses his face. "I feel better already for telling you. And thanks for the offer, but I'd rather drive myself. It'll give me some time to think. Can I trust you to stay out of trouble? At least until I get back?"

Now that's a big ask, but I'll humor him. "Of course." I circle the desk and give him a quick hug. "I'll see you tomorrow."

I hope I can uphold my promise to stay out of trouble.

I'll do my best to try.

CHAPTER 13

I'm just putting my phone away after texting
Dylan his flight information when Gage walks
into my bookstore. The look on his face isn't a happy one.
What now?

Before I can ask what's wrong, Cooper wakes from his
nap on the couch he's designated as his own and trots over to
greet Gage. My dog is like a happy switch for most people.
He's hard not to like.

Gage leans down and gives Cooper a pat. "Hey, Buddy."
Gage glances up, his face still etched with concern. "Looks
like the trust lawyers are going forward with your uncle's
filing about adding Brittany. I wish your mom had let me
take care of that situation for her. I'm still sorting through
what the lawyer from San Francisco did."

I whisper because Brittany is in the back room. "Evidently, Brittany's mother was the one who insisted on using someone from out of town. To maintain her privacy."

"How would you feel if I tracked Brittany's mother down?"

I circle the sales counter and flop on Cooper's couch. "Why? What would that do? Besides upset Brittany."

"When I went through the paperwork, I found a receipt that showed the lawyer was paid by Brittany's mother. How could she afford that? I thought she was broke."

I'm trying to remember all the details I've learned about Brittany. "I assumed my mother paid for the adoption with the money from her inherited wine. Because Brittany's mother *was* supposedly on her last dime. Brittany told me it's one of the reasons her mom ran off with a guy. But the guy didn't want a kid too, so my mom adopted Brittany."

Gage nods. "Why would Brittany's mom care about privacy if she planned to dump Brittany and leave with a guy? Something seems off there."

It really does. "Do you think my uncle might have gotten wind of Brittany living on her own and set this whole thing up? Bribing her mom and the other lawyer to do something wrong with the adoption so Uncle Frank would have the ammunition to void the trust and inherit everything?"

"That's pretty devious, even for your uncle." Gage gives Cooper a pat before he joins me on the couch. "Something isn't adding up. Maybe Brittany's mother can fill in the details. If we can find her."

"But can we believe a word the woman says?" I have serious doubts about that.

Gage shrugs. "Maybe she's out of money by now and needs more?"

Maybe. But man, I hate to open that can of worms. "Okay. Let's see if you can locate her, but we'll keep this to ourselves for now. I have to sell some wine to pay for a storefront renovation, so I'll sell enough to pay you for the search too. My uncle made it sound like the trust will be frozen until this is cleared up."

"Sounds like a plan." He sticks out a piece of paper. "Renee asked if you'd bring her these things from her home while she's a guest at the station."

I accept the list of personal items. "I guess Brittany's watch research didn't amount to anything if Dylan still arrested her."

Gage holds out a key next. "Actually, Dylan thought Renee might be safer in jail until the killer is caught. Especially after seeing how completely her life has been hacked. Renee had Ed change all her locks this morning."

Maybe Dylan believes Renee is innocent after all? "Okay, I'll go get her things now. Thanks, Gage."

"No problem." He gives Cooper one last pat. "And don't worry about paying me. I can wait until we get the trust all squared away."

I forgot he's a trust fund kid and doesn't need the money. "I appreciate that, but I'll keep current on my bills. Thanks for looking into this for me. Going to the funeral tomorrow morning?"

"Nope. Gotta work. See you around."

After Gage leaves, I poke the swinging door to the back room and call out, "Hey, Brittany? Can you close up for me? I'm going to go pick up some things for Renee."

"Yep. You still want to go to the diner for the fund-raiser later?"

"Sure. I'll text you when I'm done." I'd almost forgotten about the fund-raiser. The local theater group is raising money for their winter production. My father is going to perform in it too.

I pop out onto the sidewalk and draw in a deep breath. The mix of flowers and ocean air is something I missed when I moved away. The summertime weather is especially lovely today, not a cloud in the sky, waves crashing rhythmically against the shore as I walk toward Renee's house. But memories of the last time I was in Renee's empty house creep in, so I call Madge.

She answers, "What's up?"

"I'm heading to Renee's to pick up a few things for her stay in your lovely facility. Would you like to join me?"

Madge chuckles. "Got a case of the chickens, huh?"

I'd rather think of it as being prudent, but she's right. "If you're busy, no worries."

"Nope. It's quitting time. I'll be right there. And I'll be packing heat." She hangs up without saying goodbye.

When I arrive at Renee's house, I circle to the back. I

learned my lesson from the last time I was here and pull a tissue from my purse so I don't leave fingerprints. I tug on the sliding door. It's locked.

I make my way down the deck stairs and back to the front just as Madge's VW pulls into the driveway.

She rolls out of the car and slings her purse on her shoulder. "Renee said to bring her tablet too. It's by her bed upstairs."

"Okay." I pull the new key from my pocket and open the moaning screen door with my tissue. As I slip the key into the lock, the door opens slightly before I can turn the knob. "It wasn't locked. Gage said Ed changed the locks this morning."

"Try the knob. Is that locked?" Madge grabs the gun from her purse. "Maybe Ed didn't pull it all the way shut?"

"Yeah. That could be. It's old and sometimes sticks." I try to swivel the knob, but it's locked. And there are fresh deep grooves in the doorjamb.

The nerves tingling up my spine aren't so convinced Ed forgot to close the door all the way. He's pretty serious about security. "I'll call Ed before we go inside. He might want to see this." Since Ed installed all the cameras and new locks at my house and store recently, I have his number in my phone.

I dial and wait for his voicemail to finish before leaving a message. After I hang up, I say, "Maybe we should call one of the deputies to meet us?"

Madge shakes her head. "I have Betsey here to protect us." She lifts the gun. "I'll even go first."

A NOVEL WAY TO DIE

Since when is Madge so brave? "I don't think this is a good idea. Especially because I promised Dylan I'd stay out of trouble until he comes back. This is like those people in the horror flicks who run straight into danger." I tug on Madge's arm to stop her from opening the front door any further.

"Wait." Madge holds up her finger. "Do you hear that?"

I stand still and listen. Soft, high-pitched moaning sounds. I whisper, "Is that a cat?"

"Does Renee have any cats?"

"No." I lean my ear closer to the door. "It's definitely coming from inside. Sounds like someone's hurt. Call for help."

While Madge dials, I poke the front door open all the way but stay put. What if it's a trap of some sort? I stick my head inside, while my feet are ready to run if they have to. Nothing seems out of place in the living room. "Hello?"

Madge hangs up and stands beside me as the high-pitched moaning sounds again.

I quietly say, "We need to help whoever that is. How long before the paramedics and cops get here?" It's handy she's the dispatcher and would know this.

"Four to eight minutes, maybe fifteen if it's between shift changes." Madge adds, "Sounds like it's coming from the second floor. Grab the bat from under the stairs. Whoever that is might not have fifteen minutes."

Madge makes a good point.

I jog inside and open the closet door where the bat is kept and grab it. "Let's go."

We walk side by side up the stairs. The moaning is getting louder, so we pick up the pace. The wail of approaching sirens gives me the added confidence that help will be here any second, so I jog ahead of Madge and turn toward Renee's bedroom, where the sounds are coming from.

The door is standing open. With my bat at the ready and an extra gulp of air for courage, I creep slowly inside. A pair of familiar sparkly sneakers are sticking out beside the bed, so I pick up the pace. Angelica is sprawled on the floor, holding her head.

I quickly drop the bat and kneel by her side. First, her husband is killed, and now she's hurt? "Help's on the way, Angelica. What happened?" I don't see any blood, thankfully. It's no time for me to be passing out.

"Sawyer?" Angelica blinks her eyes open. "You're blurry. Something hit me from behind."

Madge kneels beside us too. "Help's almost here."

"Thanks." Angelica winces as she nods.

I ask before the cops come and shoo us away, "Why were you here?"

"My mom said Renee called the house. Renee wanted to tell me something about Zach. I thought it might... I feel..." Her eyes close, and she goes limp.

"Hang in there, Angelica," Madge says before she runs to the landing to direct the help, who're clomping up the stairs.

I take Angelica's hand, expecting it to feel cold and clammy, but it feels normal. Maybe that's a good sign.

The paramedics rush in, so I stand and step back. Angelica's awake again and speaking, so I swipe the tablet off the nightstand and then sneak into the bathroom to get the other things Renee asked for.

Madge slips beside me. "The deputies are here. I told them what happened, and now they want us out."

"I'm almost done. Grab that shampoo, and I'll get the rest of what Renee wanted."

Madge opens the shower door as I slide around the paramedics, who are loading Angelica on a stretcher. I snatch the clothes Renee needs, and then Madge and I head downstairs.

When we hit the front porch, Ben, the new deputy, is waiting for us.

He says, "Why are you two always in the middle of all our troubles lately?"

I shrug. "Bad luck?" I pull Madge's arm and start for her VW. "We'll get out of your hair now. We got what we need for Renee."

"Hold up, ladies." Ben pulls a little pad from his top pocket. "Tell me what happened from the moment you got here."

Madge jumps in and, in almost perfect police jargon, recounts what happened.

When she's done, I say. "Maybe you should talk to Angelica's assistant, Kate, about this. You know Renee is in custody and couldn't have made that call."

Ben frowns. "No one knows where Kate is. Dylan only told us she's somewhere safe. I'd better call him."

"Good plan. We'll run Renee's things over to her now." I know where Kate's supposed to be. But maybe I'd better not share if Dylan didn't even tell his deputies her whereabouts.

Ben nods as he dials his phone. This is our chance to sneak away. I grab Madge's arm and tug her toward her VW again.

Once inside the car, I say, "We need to go to Dylan's house before we go to the station."

"Why?" Madge starts her car and backs down the drive.

I can't tell Madge I need to see if Kate's where she's supposed to be. But I don't want to lie to Madge, so I say, "It's sort of personal."

Madge's lips tilt in a knowing grin. "Personal, huh? Are things better between you two?"

"Definitely better than when I first came back home, but not better the way your evil grin suggests."

Madge chuckles. "I'm happy with any kind of 'better' between you two."

I'm doing my best to listen as Madge blathers on about all the reasons Dylan and I are meant to be together, but my only focus is on what I'll do if Kate isn't where she's supposed to be. I guess I'd have to call Dylan to see if he moved her somewhere else.

When we get to Dylan's house, Madge asks, "Want me to wait outside?" She waggles her brows.

"That'd be great. I forgot the key, so I have to use the old window in the back that never shuts all the way." It's not as if Kate would answer the doorbell if she's supposed to be hiding out from the bad guys as Dylan suggested. I'll just peek inside the windows, verify she's inside, and then slip back to the car undetected.

Hopefully.

"Okee dokey." Madge fiddles with the radio and settles in to wait.

I hop out and open the side gate, careful to make as little noise as possible. When I get to the rear, my heart stops. Dylan has replaced all the windows and blinds—and they're all shut. Probably because Kate is supposed to be secretly hiding inside.

I need to know if Kate is in there without giving her location away to anyone else. Dylan would kill me if I compromised his case by doing that.

Tilting my head up, I study the upper floor. The master bedroom window is cracked open just an inch or two. If I can get the screen off, I could slip inside. But how to get up there? I'm too heavy to climb a gutter, and unfortunately, there aren't any convenient vines growing on the side of the house.

Doing an about-face, I see the backyard looks super tidy, filled with fruit trees and lovely rose bushes. I make my way toward the large shed in the rear where his parents used to keep tools. Maybe I can find a ladder.

I grab the knob to open the shed, but it's locked. Only a cop would lock his shed doors in Sunset Cove. There are only a shovel and a rake leaning on the outside of the building.

What to try next?

I slip to the side of the house, crossing fingers the cellar doors aren't locked as well. It's creepy and damp down there, but it has access to the kitchen above.

Wishing I had something to cover my hair from cobwebs, I head for the wooden doors. But they're locked with a shiny new padlock too—of course.

Now I'm out of options. I can't smash a window with the shovel.

As I start back for the car, I spot the side door that opens into the kitchen. It has one of those locks that needs a code. Bingo! I can ask Dylan what it is.

He should be in the air, though, so he might not get my message. But wait. Then I'd have to explain why I'd want to get inside. I'm not supposed to know about Kate staying at his house. I only know because he's a terrible liar. His red cheeks gave him away.

Can I guess the code?

After tiptoeing up the three steps, I peer inside the kitchen door's window, but the gauzy curtain makes it impossible to see clearly inside. It's getting close to dinnertime, so I need to be careful not to get caught.

The code wouldn't be anything obvious like his birthday. He already got on me for using that at my shop. Or his house address, or digits of his phone number. Or his mom's birthday. He'd pick random numbers or something no one could guess who didn't know the most intimate details of his life. Which, as far as I can tell, is no one these days. Except me.

Maybe our niece's or nephew's birthdays? I quickly type one in and then the other, but no luck.

He wouldn't use my birthday, would he?

My heartbeat accelerates as I type in the date. Maybe breaking into a cop's home will be much easier than I'd thought. I try to turn the knob, but it still doesn't budge.

I'm mildly disappointed he didn't use my birthday, but shake it off.

I'll have to get a little more creative. Next, I try his locker combination from high school, but that doesn't work. Assuming I input the right number. That was a long time ago, but we used to slip notes to each other and leave little gifts during the school day, so I was in his locker often.

It wouldn't be my old combo, would it? I was lazy and used my house numbers.

Slowly, I input my digits and then try the knob. When it turns, my heart leaps in anticipation. Partly for the sneaking around I'm about to do, but even more so because he'd use my high school combination. It's sweet.

But, back to business.

I open the side door slowly and just enough to stick my head inside. Noise, like the TV's on, is coming from the den, just on the other side of the dining room. That should be enough to know someone is home, but Dylan was in a major hurry to leave town. He could've accidentally left it on.

I need to check the den.

Like a cat burglar in the movies, I slip along the kitchen wall with my back to it, high-stepping my way across the kitchen. When I'm almost to the dining room, I lean down to see under the swinging half door. Only the legs of chairs and a table base are visible, but that door used to squeak, so I crawl under it and stay on all fours as I make my way across the hardwood floor.

My knees are screaming in pain from the hard surface, so I stop for a second under the dining room table to give them a break. While rubbing my kneecaps, I listen for any signs of a human in the next room. A sneeze or a cough would be welcome. And then I'd hightail it out the way I came.

It seems Kate is allergy-free, so I need to keep moving, darn it. My blood pressure must be through the roof because I can feel my heartbeat in my ears. As I debate staying low under the table or standing up to give my knees a break, a creak sounds.

Is it an old-house creak, or the creak of wooden floors being walked upon? Probably best to stay hidden under the dining room table.

With my eardrums ready to pop under the stress and pressure of being an untrained cat burglar, I think I hear soft footsteps coming my way. But I can't be sure.

Drawing in deep breaths, I do my best to slow the drumbeat in my ears so I can hear what's going on. When that doesn't help much, I move a little closer to the den, but still stay under the table's protection.

A loud "Meow!" sounds and scares me so badly I jump,

smacking my head on the table. It takes all my will to not scream out in pain as I roll around on the floor as quietly as I can, begging the pain in my skull to stop.

Where did the cat come from? Dylan is a dog person, as far as I know, but maybe he changed teams.

The cat seems fascinated by me and sits on its haunches to study the strange person writhing in pain under the table. "Meow?"

"Shhh," I whisper.

How do you quiet a cat? Cooper only requires attention, so I reach out and pet the cat while listening for human footsteps.

A low rumbling starts from somewhere deep inside the little black-and-white kitty. I guess petting it wasn't the best plan.

A female voice calls out, "Boots? Do you want some dinner?"

That perks the cat right up, and it dashes toward the kitchen. But that's my escape route too.

The squeak of tennis shoes on the wood floor nearby makes me crouch even lower under the table, like that'll help. I want to see the person's face so I know for sure it's Kate, but I'll settle for the best I can do.

I grab my phone and wait until the footsteps pass me by, trying to control my breathing, so she won't hear me.

After the steps begin to fade, I stick only my arm out and snap a quick picture, hoping to get a clear picture of the person from behind to see shape and hair color.

Pocketing my phone, I scoot as fast as I can to the end of the table. As soon as I hear the familiar creak of the kitchen door and the voice asking the kitty if it's hungry, I make a run for it.

My target is the garage. I can slip out the side door without making much noise. I hope.

As fast as my sore knees allow, I run to the garage, unlock the side utility door, and slip outside.

Panting, and leaning against the side of the house to catch my breath, I hold up the phone to see what I got. I shot the picture so fast that I hope it's not a blurry mess. I need evidence to prove Kate was nearby and able to hit Angelica over the head.

When the picture appears on my screen, all the air whooshes from my lungs. The image clearly shows that the person with Kate's exact hair color and sexy curves couldn't have committed the crime. At least without someone from the station knowing.

There, as big as a billboard on her ankle, is one of those trackers for house arrest. Everyone would know she left the house if she'd gone to hurt Angelica. Kate wouldn't be that stupid. She's a smart gal, from what I've uncovered.

My whole theory of who killed Zach just flew right out the window.

If Kate didn't hit Angelica over the head, then who did? And why?

CHAPTER 14

*O*nce back in Madge's car, I shut my door as quietly as I can. "All set. Let's go to the station."

"Okay." Madge starts the car and backs out of Dylan's driveway. "Did you get what you needed in there?"

"Yep." I need to change the subject before she asks what I got from his house. "Are you and the hubs going to the fundraiser at the diner tonight?"

"No. I don't care for the food. It's greasy. But I sent in my donation."

"If you change your mind, Brittany and I are going. You're welcome to join us." The greasy food is precisely why we need a new restaurant in Sunset Cove. And I'm happy to be the one providing that. But only if I can get my trust problems cleared up.

We drive in silence for a few moments until Madge says,

"Angelica's mother must eat ice cream. Everyone in town goes into Renee's shop. Wouldn't her mom know if it wasn't Renee's voice on the phone?"

That's a good point. "But Renee couldn't have made the call, right? She's been in custody since this morning."

Madge winces. "After Dylan left, we didn't actually lock the cell. She's been out to use the ladies' room down the hall and grab a snack from the machine. I was supposed to go with her, but I was busy with the phones, so I told her to go alone. But she came right back both times."

My stomach takes a dive. "So she could've made the call?"

"In theory." Madge pulls her VW behind the municipal building and parks the car. "I'll have one of the deputies get Angelica's mom's phone records. Hopefully, we can see where the call came from before Dylan gets back tomorrow."

I follow Madge up the rear stairs to the building. "I would've never thought I'd say this, but I wish you'd kept her locked up."

"Me too." Madge uses her badge to open the door, and we head down the tiled hallway to the police station. She says, "Hey, do those fancy cameras you gals have in your shops record sound too?"

"Yeah. They do, why?"

Madge's lips thin. "In one of the books I read, a hacker accessed the security files on a computer and remixed the voices."

Oh, man. I see where she's going with this. "With enough

data from the ice-cream shop's cameras, an electronic voice recording could say almost anything. All in Renee's voice."

Madge taps her nose. "Exactly."

"Who hates Renee that much?"

Madge uses her badge again to unlock the police station door after hours. "It might not be personal. Zach could've had enemies we haven't found yet, and Renee was just the easiest target because their breakup was so contentious."

I shake my head. "No, this is personal. Renee says the emails she got had way too many intimate details."

We walk to the rear outside the holding cells, where one of the deputies I don't know is watching a movie on her tablet. She's eating a burger from the diner and hasn't even noticed us. Some guard she is.

Madge pokes her shoulder. "Hey, Roberta? We need to give Renee her things."

She smiles and pauses the movie. "I have to check them out first."

Madge hands over the bag.

After Roberta's done examining the contents, she folds the top of the bag again. "I'll give these to Renee. Dylan called and said we have to keep her locked up tight from now on. No visitors. And no more field trips to the soda machines."

Madge's shoulders slump with guilt. "Okay. See you tomorrow."

Roberta nods. "Have a nice night, guys."

When we hit the hallway, I whisper, "Someone tattled to Dylan about Renee's unsupervised breaks."

"Yeah. He's not going to be happy with me when he gets back. I'll have to bake him something tonight to soften him up." Madge opens the door for us to go back to the parking lot. "See you tomorrow at the funeral. Should be interesting to see who shows up for it."

"Yes, it will. See you then." While Madge climbs into her little car, I text Brittany to tell her I'm on my way to the diner. Next, I circle the building to cross the grassy square.

Brittany is locking the doors to the bookstore, so I join her. "I thought you'd have gone home by now."

Brittany pockets her keys, and we head past all the little specialty shops to the diner. "I dropped Cooper at home and fed him, then I came back because I wanted to try something with our security cloud files. One of my friends gave me an idea to trace who hacked Renee's."

"Ah." It's a mild evening, with a light ocean breeze ruffling our hair. Too lovely an evening to be spoiled with talk about Renee's hacker, but I appreciate Brittany's dedication, so I ask, "Will it work?"

"Maybe." Brittany shrugs. "I still have a few things to figure out. I wish you guys would let me talk to Raphe. He'd be able to help us." Her forehead crumples in frustration as it does whenever we talk about Raphe lately.

I throw an arm over Brittany's shoulder and draw her close as we stroll down the sidewalk. "You really like him, don't you?"

"I guess." Her eyes cut my way before she quickly looks away again. "He's sent me like ten IMs through our game asking why I ghosted him. I hate that I can't tell him why. He's the only guy I've ever been able to stand. The rest seem so...juvenile."

Probably because Brittany had to grow up so fast. Maybe she is old enough to date—with major restrictions. "Okay, how about this? You can send him *one* message. Tell him I'm being a pain and won't let you talk to him until Zach's case is solved. You might also add something nice about how you can't wait to see him when school starts."

"I like the paranoid pain part. But no way am I saying something lame like I can't wait to see him in school."

The *paranoid* part is a little offensive. "There's nothing wrong with letting Raphe know you like him. Guys like to know where they stand."

"Oh, really?" Brittany stops walking in front of the diner and laughs. "Then how about taking your own advice? Look who's headed our way."

I'm surprised to see Dylan, who must've aborted his trip, power walking toward us, obviously on a mission. Or he's mad. It's hard to tell.

I lift my chin and cross my arms. "My situation with Dylan isn't the same as a high school crush. It's...complicated."

Brittany's chin lifts too. "Chicken?"

"No." That's the second time today I've been called that. Madge said it too. "I'll do one better than just telling him.

Watch this." I hate being called a chicken. I like to think I'm a practical person, but sometimes one has to prove words aren't just talk.

Dylan skids to a stop in front of us. "Hi, ladies. Sawyer, I need to talk to you. Please."

"Okay. After this." I slip both my hands along his cheeks and pull his face to mine. And then I kiss him. Long, slow, and with conviction.

After I release him, he leans back and grins. With unmistakable desire in his eyes, he whispers, "That wasn't what I wanted to discuss, but maybe later tonight?"

Perhaps that wasn't the best example to set for Brittany. I don't want her kissing Raphe like I just kissed Dylan to save my pride. But man, it was nice.

"Great," Brittany groans as she opens the door to the diner, "Now I've lost my appetite."

After she's inside, Dylan frowns. "What's wrong with her?"

"Nothing. Did you cancel your trip because of Angelica?"

"Yeah." Dylan opens the door and stands aside for me to go first into the land of fried everything. "That's what I want to talk to you about over a burger. My treat."

"If you're buying, then I'm getting two desserts." I smile so he knows I'm kidding.

He leans down and whispers over the din of silverware clinking and rock music blaring, "That kiss was better than any dessert they serve here."

"Behave." I poke him in the ribs as we make our way to

the red booth already occupied by my grossed-out teenage ward.

Dylan's phone rings, so he says, "I have to take this. Order for me, please." He rushes out the door to talk outside.

I slip into the booth next to Brittany. "Okay, if we join you? Or would that ruin your reputation?" The diner with its red, cracked, fake leather booths and Formica tabletops is almost full due to the fund-raiser.

She looks up from her phone. "Sadly, I have no reputation to ruin."

That's probably a good thing.

Sally, a waitress I plan to steal as soon as my restaurant is open, joins us. She's around my age, tall, thin, and reminds me of Olive Oyl, Popeye's girlfriend.

She smiles. "Hi, guys. What are we having tonight?" Sally places three glasses of water in front of us. "I saw you came in with Dylan. Assuming he's joining you?"

Sally doesn't miss a trick, even as busy as it is. And I've never seen her write down an order. Even more impressive, the food is always right when it comes out. "Yep. And be sure to give Dylan the bill. He's buying."

Brittany orders a grilled cheese and fries. I order a lone cheeseburger because my pants are getting too tight—I'll just steal some of Dylan's fries. "Dylan will have a cheeseburger with lettuce, onions, pickles, and mustard, hold the mayo and tomatoes. Large fry and a chocolate milkshake too, please."

Sally's right brow arches. "I know Dylan's usual order.

Interesting you do. I don't recall ever seeing you two here together before."

Sally didn't grow up in Sunset Cove, so she's one of the few who doesn't know my history with Dylan. It's refreshing for a change.

Before I can answer, Brittany wags her thumb at me and says, "They're together, all right. This one just sucked face with him right outside. So embarrassing. You can't take her anywhere."

"Oh." A crestfallen expression crosses Sally's face. "I'll have your order out shortly." She turns and scurries away.

I ask Brittany, "Does she have a thing for Dylan?"

She rolls her eyes with her usual teenage flair. "Every woman over twenty in town wants him. You've got him but clearly don't know what to do with him. Better hurry and figure it out before you lose him again."

Brittany always tells me I have no game when it comes to men. I think our kiss outside proved I know exactly what to do with Dylan, but I'm supposed to be parental, so I take a long drink of my ice water and stay mute.

"Sawyer, there you are!" Annie calls out as she and her husband Charlie shuffle toward us. There's a taller man with them I don't know.

I lift a hand. "Hi, guys."

Charlie tilts his chin in acknowledgment. "Got your voicemail. I'll get busy on your shop tomorrow."

"Thanks. I really appreciate it."

Annie grabs the thin, dark-haired man beside her and

maneuvers him in front of her. "Sawyer, this is Clint. He works with Angelica. Remember, I told you about him?"

Ah, the ghostwriter. He's as handsome as Annie had said. His face is Greek-god-like with sharp cheekbones and a straight nose, and he has perfect and blindingly white teeth. He's so good-looking, he's…pretty. I stand to greet them and realize he's not as tall as I thought. But then, Annie and Charlie are on the short side. "Hi. It's nice to meet you. I'm sorry it's under these circumstances."

"Yes, thank you." Clint holds out his hand. "Annie's told me so many nice things about you." Clint's voice sounds happy to meet me, but his guarded expression tells a whole different story. Annie's probably been matchmaking, spouting details about me to him ad nauseam.

"Annie spoke highly of you too." I return the handshake and stare into his mesmerizing turquoise-blue eyes. While Clint's features are sharp, his long, thin palm is softer than mine, and his manicure is nicer too. His hands are more feminine than mine. I guess pampered hands are the difference between being a writer and a chef. He makes me wish I'd moisturized better this morning.

Dylan reappears and sticks his hand out toward Clint. "Hi, I'm Sheriff Cooper." Dylan's free arm snakes around my shoulder, and he pulls me close. Like he's jealous. It's cute.

Clint quickly drops my hand and shakes Dylan's. "Sheriff. Angelica has told me how helpful you've been during this difficult time. Thank you."

Dylan forces a grin. "Just doing the job. I hear Angelica's resting at her mom's house?"

"Yes. The doctor asked us to watch for signs of a concussion but thought Angelica would be more comfortable at home. We're hopeful she'll be well enough to attend Zach's funeral tomorrow."

Dylan nods. "We're all hopeful for a fast recovery."

Charlie says, "Me too. But I'm starving, so if you'll excuse me." He heads for the only empty booth in the diner.

Annie grunts, "That man. He has the manners of a bear when he's hungry. Clint, you stay and chat." She winks at me and then hobbles behind Charlie.

"No, no." Panic flashes in Clint's eyes. "Dinner's on me. Remember, Annie?" He turns to us. "Very nice to meet you, but I need to get going. Angelica is waiting for me to bring her a burger after we eat. Bye." Clint scurries away like his fancy Italian shoes are on fire.

Brittany, who's sitting in the booth smirking, says, "See? You have no game, Sawyer."

Dylan slides into the booth across from Brittany and tugs my hand to join him on his side. He says, "Maybe Clint is in a relationship. Ever thought of that?"

"That's not it." I slip in beside Dylan. "Annie says he's single. But isn't there something strangely familiar about him? I can't put my finger on it."

Brittany shakes her head. "He's strangely good-looking, that's all."

I nod. "He's *extremely* good-looking. But not my type. I

prefer men who don't hog the bathroom mirror to style their perfect hair." I run a hand through Dylan's thick hair and muss it.

The side of his mouth quirks up. "The lack of hair gel in my house must mean I'm perfect for you."

Brittany holds up her hand. "Not to change this scintillating subject, but did you hear what Clint said? He's bringing Angelica dinner. I've had a concussion, and the last thing I'd eat was a greasy burger. I was sick to my stomach."

"Same here." Dylan takes a deep drink of his water and nods. "But I was slammed by a giant linebacker playing football." He turns to me. "What did you see when you found her? Ben said there wasn't a weapon at the scene."

"She was on the floor by Renee's bed, holding the back of her head. Angelica's hair didn't have any blood that I could see, thankfully. I didn't feel for a bump because the paramedics were coming."

"Mmm. Maybe she didn't get hit hard enough to have a full-blown concussion." Dylan drinks some more water and then says, "I wish Renee had one of those doorbell cameras at her house like I do. Then we'd know what happened." His eyes lock with mine.

Darn it! Why didn't I think to look for cameras at his house? I'm so busted. But I don't want to fight in front of the kid. "Hey, Brittany? I noticed you didn't order a milkshake. You love them. Why don't you run and ask Sally to add one to our order?"

"I thought milkshakes qualified as junk food." Brittany

looks at Dylan and then back at me. "You're trying to get rid of me, right?"

"Yep. After you order, go outside and call Raphe. Tell him only what we discussed. But make it quick."

Brittany slides out of the booth. "I'll skip the shake but make the call. Take your time." She fake-smiles at us then saunters out the door.

When she's out of earshot, I say, "Sorry about breaking into your house. I needed to know Kate was where she was supposed to be. Angelica told me about the call to her mom that was supposedly from Renee."

"I'm not mad about that. Actually, I'm a little impressed you remembered the code." He slips an arm on the back of the booth and faces me. "But what did it prove?"

Whispering, I say, "It blew my whole theory out of the water about Kate being the chief suspect." I look away and play with my straw wrapper. "I still think Raphe might have been involved, but I'm not sure how."

Dylan leans closer and whispers back, "You have a chink in your logic. Because Kate was where she was supposed to be doesn't mean she couldn't have made that call. She could have an accomplice. Anyone could have, even Angelica, even though we know she never left the signing. You can't rule anyone out at this point."

Hope swells inside again. "So you agree with me about Kate being a suspect? And that Renee didn't make the call even though it was her voice, apparently?"

His fingers massage the back of my neck. "I didn't say

that at all. I just wanted to point out possibilities. No matter who made the call, why send Angelica to Renee's house? Did we miss something someone was after, or was Angelica simply there to be injured? Or worse, killed?"

"Maybe Angelica knows more than she's letting on? Like maybe she knew about Kate and Zach's affair. Was she looking for proof to see if Zach was cheating with Renee too, and someone followed her?" I've been dying to know if Angelica suspected the affair. I hold my breath and hope Dylan will finally spill.

Instead, he frowns. "Renee would've never sent you to her house to pick up those things and then call and ask Angelica to meet her. Even if she had an accomplice to hurt Angelica. She'd never risk you being a witness. Makes zero sense."

"Exactly! Whoever made that call didn't know Renee had been locked up or that I was going to her house." I start to lift my hand for a high five but stop. "That's why you locked Renee up, isn't it? To help prove she didn't kill Zach?"

"My employees letting her roam the halls didn't help that plan." The smirk on his face tells me I'm right.

I should have trusted Dylan knew Renee would never hurt anyone. "So now what? Do we let Kate come to the funeral tomorrow and see what happens between her and Angelica? Or maybe—"

"Maybe." Dylan holds up a hand. "You just let me do my job? How about that novel concept?"

Brittany reappears across from us. "Are you two done

fighting? I need to tell you something I found out from Raphe."

Dylan and I both lean closer to hear Brittany's news over the diner's loud music, just as Sally appears with our burgers.

She hands Dylan's over first. "Just the way you like it." She smiles sweetly at him and then quickly sets mine and Brittany's in front of us. "Anything else you'd like, Dylan?" She stares at him and waits for the innuendo in her question to set in.

"Nope." He shifts in the seat and forces a smile. "Looks like we're all set here. Thanks."

Sally huffs out a breath and nods. "Enjoy your meals." She turns and hurries away.

There are so many questions I'd like to ask Dylan about that encounter, but Brittany's news needs to come first. Irritation at Brittany for speaking to Raphe about the specifics of the case when I told her not to wars with my joy at possible new information she might have found. "I thought we'd agreed you'd keep Raphe out of this?"

She nods. "I did. I swear. I told him I couldn't talk to him until after Zach's murder had been solved. I was going to hang up, but then he said he needed to tell me something." Brittany looks around to see if anyone is listening before she leans forward and says, "It was probably Raphe who changed Renee's watch data. But when he did it, he didn't know it was her data. He was just helping some old guy."

Dylan asks, "What old guy?"

"A guy came into the ice cream store a few months ago

and was messing around with his smartwatch and his laptop. When Raphe delivered his ice cream to the table, the man asked if Raphe could help him figure something out. Said he didn't want his wife to know he'd stopped for a treat because he wasn't supposed to have stuff like that since his heart attack."

Dylan nods. "So Raphe helped the guy?"

"Yeah. The man said if he doesn't walk or ride his bike every day enough, his wife gets on him. He wanted Raphe to show him how to fudge the data now and then. It was all innocent as far as Raphe was concerned. The guy offered him a hundred bucks, but Raphe said he'd do it for free because he felt bad the guy couldn't have some ice cream sometimes."

"So what happened next?" Dylan asks.

"The man gave Raphe his cloud email to change the data, tipped him a twenty, and said there'd be more the next time because he had one more date to change. The guy came in a few days later, watched Raphe make the changes, and then gave him a hundred bucks in cash and left. Raphe's never seen him again. But Raphe heard from our mutual friends I was looking into a similar thing. That's when he put two and two together. It's what he's been trying to contact me about."

Dylan sighs. "Thanks for telling us right away. Hopefully, we'll find the man in the ice cream store's video footage."

Brittany says, "If it hasn't been erased from the cloud storage. It'd be the first thing I'd do."

"Right." Dylan takes a massive bite of his burger and

chokes it down. "I'd better go talk to Raphe now. See if he can help retrieve that data." Dylan throws two twenties on the table.

"I'll go with you." Brittany dumps her barely touched sandwich onto her plate.

"No!" Dylan and I say in unison.

I beat Dylan to the explanation, "We still don't know how deeply Raphe's involved. It could be dangerous for you. Finish your dinner, please." I stand to let Dylan slide out. "Want me to get you a to-go box?"

He shakes his head. "See you tomorrow." He gives my arm a squeeze on his way by and then heads for the front door at a jog.

After I sit down again, Brittany says, "At least let me tell Raphe we need him to be at the funeral tomorrow."

I don't want her involved with Raphe any more than necessary, but on the other hand, Raphe's the only one who's possibly seen the killer. That is, if Raphe isn't involved too somehow.

"Okay. Do it."

CHAPTER 15

ressed in black, Brittany and I enter the funeral parlor. The sweet smell of lilies makes me wince, reminding me that I was here just a few months ago, attending my mom's funeral. A wave of sadness leaves a lump in my throat.

When I glance at Brittany, she has tears in her eyes.

I whisper, "You don't have to do this."

"I'm good." Brittany blinks away her tears and pops in her earbuds. After she messes with her phone, she gives me a slight nod to indicate she's ready to film and record.

Madge hustles toward us wearing a dark dress and low black heels, sans a Christmas sweater for the first time since I've returned home.

She says, "You guys ready for this?" Madge pats her purse to remind us she's packing heat, as promised.

Brittany and I both nod to Madge as a man in a dark suit holds out a program and quietly directs us into the room where Zach's service will be held. The program says there's going to be a lunch reception to follow. That'll make it easier to mingle and eavesdrop on conversations.

Fellow book club members, the Admiral, Julie, and Nick, are already seated in the back row, so the three of us join them. As quiet organ music fills the air, I look around to see who's already seated. The funeral parlor employees glide silently about, directing people to their seats. I remember thinking at my mom's funeral that the people who work here must take the same training as those high-class butlers who slip in and out of rooms without being noticed. It's disturbing and slightly creepy. But, back to proving Renee is innocent.

I'm looking for three people. An older man who talked to Raphe in the ice-cream shop, a woman with Renee's build who owns a smartwatch like Mr. Martinez spotted, and perhaps someone with muscles who could be Kate's accomplice.

In the front row, Zach's parents are hunched over, his mother's shoulders shaking in grief. Angelica is seated with her parents and her brother on the opposite side of the aisle. Angelica is wearing dark sunglasses and a big black hat. She probably still has a killer of a headache. Clint, dressed in a slick black suit, arrives with a glass of water and holds it out for Angelica as his eyes scan the seats. When he sees me, he nods, and then his eyes carry on their perusal of the room. Is he thinking what I am? That somewhere, seated in blue-upholstered metal chairs, could be the person who killed Zach?

With a shiver still lingering up my spine, I turn my attention to the front. The casket, a gleaming shiny wood number, is closed. I suppose this is because of Zach's head injuries. There are numerous huge bouquets of flowers, and it looks like Angelica spared no expense. As it should be. Her books have been on the top of the bestseller lists for years. Is it wrong that the chef in me wonders who's catering the food afterward?

Yes, it's terrible. I need to focus.

The people behind Zach's folks are mostly locals. My uncle Frank is in the third row, sitting beside his assistant, creepy psychic Beth. He's whispering something to the head of our merchants' association, Joe Kingsley, seated on his other side. They're probably plotting how they'll run me out of town soon. Behind them are some of our teachers from high school. Ice cream store employees, Raphe, Z, and Annie, and her husband, Charlie, are here too. Along with a few of our classmates, all grown up now and looking sad. It's odd to lose someone in their early thirties. It makes one face one's own mortality straight on.

There are people in the rows behind Angelica who look like business associates, dressed for board meetings rather than the funeral of a friend. Maybe they're publishing people. Most of them have watches similar to Renee's, so that's not going to help. As a matter of fact, half the room has fancy smartwatches.

A woman dripping in gold with big hair and a phone plastered to her ear—who is not wearing a smartwatch—is talking loudly enough I recognize her voice as Angelica's agent. She's talking about a press release that will go out only after Zach's funeral. How they've managed to keep the news quiet up to now so Angelica can grieve in private is interesting.

Me? I'd want the world to know someone killed my husband. Maybe someone out there knows something that could help Dylan solve the case. But then, I'm not a famous author. Perhaps privacy is what she needs for just a short time before Angelica will be expected to make public comments about something so painful.

In the next few rows are some local townspeople, including Mr. Martinez. And in the seat behind him, a familiar curvy blonde has just taken her place next to a rumpled-looking man in khakis and a plaid short-sleeved shirt. Is that Kate? Did she come wearing her ankle bracelet? Or did Dylan let her off for the day? I strain to get a peek and see there's no tracking device on her leg.

Madge's elbow pokes my ribs as she whispers, "Kate showed up? That's some nerve. Bet she's packing heat too!"

"Let's hope not." Why would Dylan hide Kate away at his house and then let her roam freely around the funeral? It makes no sense.

The officiant has entered in the front and looks at his

notes. Next, the rear doors close, and Dylan and four of his deputies take their places around the perimeter of the room like they're expecting trouble.

Renee suddenly appears in the seat next to mine and gives me a shoulder bump.

I whisper, "What are you doing here?"

The organ music abruptly stops, so Renee can't answer. Instead, she mouths, *Tell you later.*

Tell me what later? This sends my overactive imagination into hyperdrive. But I guess I'll have to wait to find out what's going on.

AFTER ZACH'S father is done tearfully eulogizing about what an incredible son Zach was, he sits again, and the minister declares the service over. Quiet organ music resumes as all the guests slowly shuffle to an adjoining room where, apparently, the food is set up. The book club members, all in the last row, wait patiently until it's our turn to exit.

Dylan appears and takes Renee's hand. "If you'll excuse us, I need Renee with me." They both exit out the back doors.

Great. Now I have no idea what they're up to. Will it interfere with the book club's mission? Obviously, we don't want to get in the way of anything Dylan has planned.

The Admiral whispers, "It's showtime, folks. Let's split up and see what we can learn. We should reconvene at the bookstore after to compare notes."

Julie whispers, "I have to get back to the grocery store. Good luck, everyone." She hands me her Taser flashlight. "Sorry I couldn't help."

Then Nick says, "Yeah. The mayor said we could attend the service, but then we had to get right back to work. I bet he stays for a sandwich, though. See you, guys." He hands me his Taser too. "I installed the camera behind Renee's store. I'll send you any activity alerts."

So that just leaves Madge, the Admiral, and Brittany. Maybe that's for the best with whatever Dylan has planned.

The Admiral says, "We didn't need those mutineers anyway. We'll be more efficient and less obvious without them. Let's go."

I exchange a glance with Madge. The Admiral isn't the most reliable source of information and is easily distracted, so I tilt my head in his direction.

Madge gets the hint and says, "I'll be your partner, Admiral." She joins him, and they make their way into the reception room while Brittany and I follow behind. One whole side of the soothing pale-yellow room is filled with food. There are dainty sandwiches, fruit salads, quiches, and meat and cheese trays galore. Above the table are blown-up pictures of Zach from childhood up until recently. It's heartbreaking.

The Admiral says, "Oh look, there's cake. Let's go!" He and Madge head happily to the pretty dessert table filled with pastries that look like they've been created by an extremely talented French chef. They fill their plates to the brim and dig in, oblivious to what's going on around them.

Brittany whispers, "And now we've lost two more."

"Yep." I guess the surveillance is up to Brittany and me.

I glance around the room, searching for our first target. Kate, without her ankle bracelet, is talking with Annie and Charlie. Kate's sipping coffee, pretending to listen as she carefully watches Angelica out of the corner of her eye. Angelica has removed her sunglasses and is discreetly checking out Kate as Angelica speaks with her agent and Clint.

Kate could be a good place to start. Maybe we can join Annie and Charlie and see what Kate's talking about.

"What are you two up to?" Dylan's voice says in my ear. "And why is Raphe here?"

I wrap an arm around Brittany and plaster on an innocent expression. "Us? We're just people-watching. Raphe's doing the same. Where's Renee?"

"Busy." He crosses his arms. "Whatever you think you're doing, please stay away from her and Kate. And tell Raphe to go home."

Brittany stops pretending to be bored and says, "Why?"

"Because I said so." He turns and walks away.

Before I can roll my eyes, Brittany beats me to it, so I lift my hand for a low five. "Since we're banned from Kate, I'll talk to the rumpled guy sitting next to her during the service. Why don't you go hang out by the food table and see what you can overhear from all those people in the business suits."

"Got it." Brittany heads out to take her position but stops. "What about Raphe? Want me to tell him to leave?"

"He's probably had enough time to look at faces anyway, so I'll tell him he can go. After I do something first."

Swiveling my head back and forth, I'm looking for the man who sat next to Kate during the service. He's like "one of those things that just doesn't belong." He wasn't dressed in dark clothing like everyone else, and he seemed to be more interested in his phone than the service. Why is he here?

I search the people in line for the food but don't see him, so I head for the dessert table where the Admiral and Madge are still indulging in sweets, talking to each other. Where did that khaki-pants guy go? I don't see him anywhere. Did he leave?

Just as I'm about to give up and pick a new person to stalk, I spot Khaki Pants. He's on his cell, lingering near a hallway that, according to the sign above, leads to the restrooms. A quick glance to the left shows Brittany is busy doing her job. She's looking bored just as we'd planned, so I lean toward Madge and whisper, "Keep an eye on Brittany for a few minutes, please. I'll be right back."

Madge just nods because her piehole is filled with cake, so I hightail it toward the mystery man. I want to hear what he's talking about.

Pretending to need the facilities, I smile as I pass by him, and then take a few steps down the hallway and stop. I lean against the wall just outside the ladies' room doorway so I can hear what the man is saying.

He's making a lot of "um-hmm" sounds and "yeah," which are doing me zero good. I don't know how long I can stand here without being caught, but I want to wait it out just a few more minutes.

Finally, the rumpled guy says, "Has Clint's role been confirmed yet? I heard him introduced as a family friend."

I lean closer to hear better. Why would this guy be asking about Clint?

It's quiet for a few more moments until he says, "Yeah. But they're all rumors. I need a solid second source. Could be sour grapes I'm hearing."

Solid source? Is he a reporter? Kate seemed to know him. When she came in, she aimed for the seat next to him. Is Kate selling a story to get back at Angelica? Maybe about Clint being a ghostwriter? I heard Angelica's agent tell someone specifically that there weren't going to be any statements until after the funeral.

The door to the bathroom opens, and my uncle's personal psychic walks out.

Great. She's all I need right now. "Hi, Beth."

Her brow crumples. "Are you waiting to talk to me?"

If Beth were really a psychic, wouldn't she know that? "No, I was just…waiting for the bathroom."

"There's like five stalls you can go in." Beth blinks her eyes rapidly like there's something in them, and then she shivers. "Can't you just feel the evil in the air?"

I'm trying to listen in on the phone call, but I think Khaki

Pants must've hung up, so I turn my attention back to Beth. "Not particularly."

Beth leans down and whispers, "Did you change your mind about wanting to know who hit the golf ball through your store's window?"

Why not? I'll play along. "Yes, actually. I'd love to know who did that."

"So you only believe in my powers when it's convenient for you?" Beth's expression turns smug.

I don't have time for this. "If you don't know, that's fine. I need to get back."

"I knew you were lying about needing the restroom." Beth's right brow arches.

Brother. I want to ask if her first clue was when I didn't go inside the bathroom. But my mom taught me better manners than that. "See you around." I turn and have to stop myself from running. Beth always makes me nervous and jumpy.

Beth calls out, "It was Raphe."

I stop and turn around. "Raphe? Why would he do that?"

Beth walks past me rubbing her fingers together. "Money will make some people do just about anything."

Wait a minute. The same kid who didn't want to take money from the old guy in the ice-cream shop took money to vandalize my bookstore? That makes no sense. But then, maybe Beth is just tugging my chain.

Or Raphe made up the story about the old man in the ice-cream shop to cover his tracks if he gets caught. He heard from their friends that Brittany was looking into Renee's watch data.

Should I tell Brittany about this or not? I'm for sure going to tell Dylan. Right now.

Feeling a little sick to my stomach that the kid Brittany likes is a rotten one, I head back out to join the others.

Madge and the Admiral are still glued to their spots eating desserts, so I check on Brittany. But I can't find her. Now I do have a bad feeling. One that has nothing to do with Beth's woo-woo stuff.

Jogging over to Madge, I grab her arm midbite. "Where's Brittany?"

Madge mumbles around her cake, "There." She points with her icing-filled fork.

I spin around and see Brittany waving to Raphe as he disappears through the doors. She must've relayed Dylan's message to Raphe. My feet start moving before my brain has figured out what I'll do when I catch up to Raphe, but I want some answers.

Besides, I can't allow him anywhere near Brittany, and I'm going to tell him that when I catch up with him.

As I pass by, I call out to Brittany. "Stay right there."

Brittany looks at me like I've lost my mind as I push the glass door open and head down the thickly carpeted hallway. As I round the corner to head for the parking lot, hoping Raphe hasn't had too big a head start on me, I halt in my tracks. By the double front doors, Clint is handing Raphe some money.

Slamming my back against the wall, I slide myself behind a fake ficus tree, straining to hear. I can't make out all the words. Clint's voice says, "Painful" and "Quickly," and then Raphe says something like "On it. Right back." And then the front door opens and the chimes sound.

Could Clint and Raphe be working together? Maybe Clint recruited Raphe to help frame Renee. But why? Could Clint have wanted Angelica all to himself? He looked at her with sincere concern when he handed Angelica that glass of water earlier. And he was in a hurry to get home to her last night with a burger. Maybe that's why he wanted nothing to do with Annie's matchmaking? Because he's in love with his cowriter?

Clint's soft, muffled footsteps are coming my way.

What am I going to do? I can't just pop out and start walking. Suddenly appearing from behind a tree is a pretty glaring clue that I've been spying on him. What if he's dangerous? Khaki Pants was pretty interested in Clint.

I grab my phone, place it against my ear, and say, "No, I haven't heard of that author. But I'll be happy to see if I can find that book when I get back to my store this afternoon."

A startled Clint stops and stares at me. Does he suspect that I saw whatever deal he was making with Raphe?

My hand shakes a little as I tuck my phone away. "Hi. Didn't want to take that inside. Seemed rude."

"Right." He nods, but his perfect face and forehead crumple like he's puzzled. "Going back in now?"

I'd wonder too why someone would hide behind a fake

tree to make a business call. "Yes. In a second. I need to make another call." But like an idiot, I just stuffed my phone in my pocket, so I take it back out. "Just remembered I need to call my sister."

"Okay." The doubt in his eyes is either for my fake phone call, or he's questioning my sanity.

I glance down and pretend to dial my sister's number, hoping he bought my story. Or, he can think I'm crazy— either works for me.

His retreating footsteps allow me to breathe somewhat normally again. After giving Clint enough time to rejoin the reception, I tuck my phone into my pocket and head back to the gathering to find Dylan.

When I open the door, a loud scream startles me. Angelica is shouting at Renee and Kate. Something about how they have the nerve to show their faces and ruin Zach's memorial.

Everyone else in the room is silent, waiting for Renee's and Kate's responses.

Brittany is standing just off to the side of the altercation. I slip beside her and ask, "How long has this been going on?"

Brittany places a finger on her lips and lifts her phone to remind me she's recording.

Nodding, I move closer to help Renee if it becomes necessary. Angelica is red-faced with anger. Who knows what she'll do in her grief-ridden state?

Dylan is standing near Angelica, absorbing the situation. His levelheadedness is what makes him a good sheriff. Clint is holding Angelica's upper arms, as if ready to restrain her if need be.

Renee softly says, "I loved him too, Angelica."

Angelica's eyes nearly bug out of her head. "So if you couldn't have him, then neither can I? Is that why you lured him to your shop and killed him?"

A collective gasp fills the air.

Renee, as calm as I've ever seen her, says, "I didn't kill him. I never stopped loving him."

I knew this, but I'd never heard Renee say it out loud. It breaks my heart.

Kate's head whips in Renee's direction, and she says, "Is that why you two were making plans to get back together again? I found the texts and emails."

Or Kate sent those texts and emails.

"What?" Angelica lunges for Renee, "Is that true?"

Clint stops Angelica's forward progress before her fist can conncct with Renee's face. He leans his mouth next to Angelica's ear and whispers something none of us can hear. Still, Angelica is one-hundred-percent focused on Renee.

Renee takes a step back and shakes her head. "I would've never taken him back. But maybe you ought to ask this one about her relationship with your husband." Renee tilts her thumb in Kate's direction, and all heads in the room swivel the same way.

Kate crosses her arms and says, "He didn't love you, Angelica. He loved me."

The hate in Angelica's eyes is chilling as she growls, "You

were too stupid to know he was just using you to make me jealous. It was an old trick he'd done before. He was never going to leave me. It was his cowardly way of getting you to quit so he didn't have to fire you. He was never going to run away with you."

So Angelica knew about Zach and Kate's affair? Or is she guessing based on what Zach had done in the past? This is so confusing.

Before Kate can answer, Raphe walks through the door and heads our way. He's holding a white bag in his hand and moving fast. Like he's on a mission.

I'd almost forgotten about the exchange in the hallway with Clint. I need to stop whatever "painful" thing Raphe is planning.

Before I can talk myself out of it, I lunge at Raphe to grab the bag. Instead, I knock us both to the floor in a painful, tangled heap. The paper bag flies a few feet away, so I crawl on my aching arms and legs and grab it.

I still see stars as I lift the bag and scream, "Dylan! Help!"

CHAPTER 16

I'm holding Raphe's white bag above my head when Dylan appears and takes whatever Raphe brought to the funeral from my hand.

"What's going on, Sawyer?" Dylan asks as he helps me stand.

"Ask him." I point to Raphe, who is sitting on the floor, rubbing his head and looking confused.

Dylan opens the bag, peers inside, and asks Raphe, "What's this all about?"

Raphe shrugs. "Clint asked where he could get some ibuprofen for Angelica's headache. I told him I'd get it for him." Raphe digs into his pocket and grabs some money. "Here's your change, Clint."

What? I stick my hand into the bag and pull out the bottle of pain relievers. Man, did I just screw up. Big-time.

Everyone is looking at me now like I'm insane. "I...um... overheard..." I turn to Raphe. "I'm sorry I knocked you down. But I'd just learned you were the one who sent a golf ball through my store's window, and then I misunderstood what you and Clint were talking about. I thought people here were in danger."

Raphe winces as he stands. "I did hit the ball through the window, but Mr. Kingsley said you wouldn't be mad because you were going to remodel the front anyway. He said he'd take care of it."

Mr. Kingsley? The head of the merchants' association? Not surprisingly, he's nowhere to be found all of a sudden. And neither is my uncle, who was probably in on the plot too.

Dylan hands the white bag to Clint and then turns to Raphe. "Explain."

"It was an accident. I swear." Raphe shoves both hands into his front pockets. "I was chipping balls in the park after dinner one night. Practicing because I want to make the golf team in the fall. I didn't have enough money to practice at the golf course, you know?"

Dylan nods. "Hitting golf balls in the park isn't allowed, but go on."

Raphe shuffles his feet nervously. "It was after most of the shops were closed, and I was just doing short chip shots so no one could get hurt. And then Mr. Kingsley comes rushing toward me. I figured I was in trouble, so I started packing up all my gear."

I can't help but ask, "Does that include all your golf balls with threats written on them?"

Raphe's forehead creases. "I don't know what you're talking about."

Dylan says, "We'll get back to that. What happened next?"

"Mr. Kingsley wasn't mad at me. He said he'd been watching me, and he thought I was pretty good. He told me how he sponsors the golf team and said he wanted to give me a few tips." Raphe pauses and searches everyone's faces. "He had some clubs and a box of balls with him. Said he wanted to see what I could do with longer shots."

Dylan asks, "So you'd put all your golf balls away at this point?"

Raphe nods. "Yeah. His were brand-new. I figured it was okay to try a few longer shots because it was getting late, and there weren't many people in the park. Then Mr. Kingsley said he wanted me to try a whole new grip on the club and to move my feet a certain way. It felt all wrong, but I heard he used to be one of the best golfers in town until shoulder surgery made him quit playing. I thought I should give the changes a try. So, I took a huge swing, but the ball sliced and went through the bookstore's window. I'm really sorry, Sawyer."

I don't know if I should believe him or not. "You have to keep your eye on the ball to hit it, right?"

Raphe nods. "Yeah."

"And you didn't notice something written on the ball?"

"No. I promise." Raphe holds up his hands. "The grass was

sort of long, though, so something could've been on the bottom, I guess. Mr. Kingsley said he'd take care of the window and not to mention it again. So, I didn't." Raphe turns to Brittany. "You have to believe me."

Dylan and I exchange a glance. The threat on the ball, which actually wasn't totally legible after Cooper slobbered on it, was only written on one side of the ball. We could barely make out my name and the "go home" part.

Dylan motions to his deputy Ben to join us. "Raphe, tell your parents I'll be over later to speak to them. Ben will talk to Mr. Kingsley, and then we'll all meet after that."

"Okay." Raphe says to me, "Maybe I can work at the bookstore to pay off the cost of the window, Sawyer. I really am sorry."

"We'll figure it out." I think Mr. Kingsley is going to have some serious explaining to do. "I'm sorry I tackled you."

"It's all good." Raphe rubs a hand up and down his arm. "You hit pretty hard for a..." Raphe's eyes go big like he just figured out he's about to dig himself into a deeper hole. "I mean for someone as...um..."

Dylan fills in the awkward silence, "For someone who's a chef and not an athlete. *At all.*" He nudges Raphe toward the door. "See you later, Raphe."

After Raphe leaves, people go back to mingling and eating again, so I whisper to Dylan, "I'm a *little* athletic. Sometimes. Do we believe Raphe or not?"

"Not sure yet. But your timing stinks, Sawyer." His jaw tics like he's angry.

"I thought I was stopping something potentially bad from happening. What's so wrong with that?"

Dylan slips his hand around my upper arm and tugs me to a quiet corner. "I put Kate, Renee, and Angelica in the same room for a reason. I was hoping someone would tip their hand. But tackling a kid put an end to all that. While we were sorting out your golf ball problems, Angelica and Clint left."

"Oh. Sorry." I gaze into his hardened stare. "I didn't mean to ruin your plans."

"I know." Dylan runs a hand down his face. "I have to get Renee and Kate secured again. And then I have a golf ball mystery to solve. See you later." He shakes his head and walks away.

Feeling horrible for what I've done, I'm even more determined to make it up to Dylan. Maybe we have some clues in the recordings Brittany made. No better time than the present to figure that out.

BACK AT MY BOOKSTORE, Madge, Brittany, the Admiral, and I all settle in the kitchen area with coffee and croissants to talk about what we learned at the funeral. Although, I'm pretty sure Madge and the Admiral only learned how tasty the pastries at the funeral were.

I start. "Did you guys notice the man sitting next to Kate at the service? I overheard him talking on the phone. I think he might be a reporter. He was looking at Clint for something."

The Admiral sets his mug down. "Could it be Angelica's ghostwriting secret? That'd make for interesting news. Especially because I've noticed it's been going on for years. What if Zach had threatened to reveal that? It could potentially hurt Angelica's career, right? Maybe someone in the publishing world killed Zach to stop the secret from coming out."

Madge says, "I'm not so sure. I learned from one of the deputies that Angelica and Zach's prenup allows Zach money from Angelica's books. It seems it wouldn't behoove Zach to reveal that secret."

I turn to Brittany. "Did your recordings of the business-people pick up anything?"

"Yeah." Brittany lays down the phone she's messing with. "They were talking about Clint. Wondering if something was going on between him and Angelica."

"So maybe the people in suits suspect the ghostwriting secret too?"

The Admiral lifts a finger. "Based on what Annie told me earlier, Angelica writes parts of her books, and so does Clint, so they might have a split payment of some sort with her publisher. It might not be a secret among her editors. But the public still believes only Angelica is writing the books. Clint's name doesn't appear anywhere."

I grab my mug and pour more French roast from the carafe on the table. "Well, Zach was having an affair with

Kate, so maybe those people wondered if Clint and Angelica were also having an affair? But Angelica said Zach was only using Kate like he'd done with other women. She didn't seem shocked to hear Zach had been cheating. Maybe none of this has anything to do with Zach's murder."

Madge nods. "But who would benefit from Zach's death? Zach and Angelica's prenuptial agreement would have left Zach with a pretty substantial settlement. Still, it wouldn't break the bank for Angelica. Nothing that would seem to stand in the way of either of them divorcing and remarrying. Certainly nothing to kill for."

I add, "And why lure Angelica to Renee's house? I'm wondering if Madge and I interrupted an attempted murder. He or she could've slipped out while we were waiting for help to arrive. Dylan didn't have all those deputies at the service for nothing. Was he trying to protect Angelica?" And how badly did I ruin Dylan's chances to catch the killer?

Brittany says, "I noticed there was a deputy near Angelica the whole time. What if he was protecting her from Clint? Maybe Clint wanted to have his name on the books too, and Zach, being the business manager, said no? We know Angelica didn't kill Zach, but do we know where Clint was during the crime?"

We all turn to Madge because she knows everything the deputies know.

She says, "I have no idea. What I do know is that Clint didn't arrive until late yesterday afternoon. After Angelica got hit on the head. I asked Angelica's mom about him at the service over a piece of that amazing cake. She said he'd driven straight here from Tahoe yesterday. He'd been visiting his mother for the weekend, evidently"

So, Madge was actually paying attention and doing her job at the funeral?

I ask, "Clint lives in San Francisco, right?"

"Yeah." Madge finishes off her second croissant and wipes the crumbs from her fingers. "I've got to get back. I'll let you guys know what I find out about Clint's whereabouts the night of the murder. And I'll have the deputies look into his credit card information. He might've stopped for gas or something, so we can confirm he wasn't in town when Angelica got whacked on the head."

"Good idea." After I drain my mug, I add, "Call me when you figure it all out."

"Will do. Bye, guys." Madge heads toward the door in her usual rush.

After Madge is gone, the Admiral says, "Speaking of Clint. Brittany, you were closest, did you hear what Clint said to Angelica to calm her during that tiff with Kate and Renee? Whatever it was seemed to work instantly."

"No, but maybe I can enhance the recording. I'll work on that this afternoon." A smirk forms. "I should also edit that film of Sawyer tackling Raphe. Make it slow motion and add some music. It'd get thousands of hits online."

I narrow my eyes. "Are you saying you'd like to make your own dinner for the rest of your life?"

"It might be worth it." Brittany stands and heads for the computer at the front desk. "I'll have to think about it."

"Yeah, well, think good and hard, my friend."

The Admiral smiles as he stands too. "It's nice to see you two acting like sisters. It'd make your mother happy, Sailor. Let me know if I can help in any way. Good luck with Joe Kingsley and your golf ball problem too. Never liked that guy."

"Thanks." One more thing to deal with today. "I'll keep you in the sleuth loop."

"Appreciate it. Bye, ladies." He turns and heads out the door.

After he's gone, Brittany says, "For the record, I believe Raphe."

"You like Raphe too much to be impartial. And just to be clear, you still need to stay away from him."

"Yeah, yeah. I know." Brittany's fingers start tapping keys on the computer. "But when Raphe is cleared, are you going to let me date him?"

Ugh. I was hoping to put off this conversation. Can I get away with just saying "we'll see" like my mom always did? No, I hated that. I need to be straight with Brittany. "*Assuming* he's cleared of any wrongdoing, and *assuming* you agree to some basic rules, I think it'd be okay for you guys to date."

"Rules?" Brittany's fingers stop tapping keys. "What kind of rules?"

My mind races with thoughts of how Dylan and I used to

sneak into the city, and all the ways we got around his curfew, as I slowly walk to the counter. In the end, I think Madge's rules with her girls make the most sense. "You have to be home at an agreed-upon time, always tell me where you're going, and answer my texts immediately. Mess any of those up, and you'll lose dating privileges."

Brittany's face scrunches up like she'd sucked a lemon. "What's my curfew, and why would you text me while I'm on a date?"

"Just to be obnoxious, of course. And I think ten is a good time to be home."

Brittany's shoulders slump in defeat. "Ten? Fourth graders go to bed at ten on Friday nights, Sawyer. Geez."

I'll use the negotiation tactics I learned in college and stay silent. Let her stew a bit.

And hope those tactics actually work.

After a few moments of muttering, Brittany crosses her arms in defiance. "Make it twelve, and you got a deal."

Of course she's going to counteroffer, just like my class said the opponent would. Luckily, I'm in the power position here. I think. "This isn't a negotiation."

Brittany throws her hands up in the air. "Ten doesn't work for anything we can even do on a date."

I pretend to be busy straightening books on a coffee table so I won't cave. "What's that supposed to mean?"

Brittany circles the counter and stands in front of me to plead her case. "The second showings of movies at the theater aren't even done by ten. Bowling and putt-putt are the same. Only old people and kids go to the six o'clock sessions of anything." She flops into the chair by the table. "I'll just tell Raphe to forget it. It'd be too embarrassing to tell him we have to eat dinner at four with the geriatric crowd to comply with your dumb rules." Brittany huffs out a breath and then launches herself out of her chair. She goes back to the computer and gets busy again. All the pounding makes me fear for the keyboard's safety.

Maybe the kid has a point. I pull out my phone and peruse movie times online. Our little theater only has two screens and two showings in the evenings.

She's right, there's no way she could be home by ten if she goes to the second movie. Next, I look at the websites for the bowling alley and the minigolf /arcade where the kids hang out. Same story. It's not reasonable. I'm being overprotective.

But still, she's only fifteen. She'd be hanging out where the older kids gather, and that could lead to trouble. But at some point, I guess I just need to trust her. It isn't like a kid can't get into trouble at all hours of the day if that's what they want to do.

With that discomforting thought still lingering, I head to the counter, where Brittany won't look at me. If it were possible for steam to shoot from someone's ears, I'm pretty sure that's what I'd be seeing right now. I'm reminding myself how every obstacle at her age seemed like it was going to cause the end of the world, so I'm trying my best to be patient. "You made a good argument for a later curfew."

Brittany's head whips up, and she blinks at me. "So, I can come home at twelve?"

"No. Eleven. Anything later will require further negotiations."

A big grin lights her face. "Thanks, Sawyer."

"And no driving anywhere outside of Sunset Cove. Deal?" I stick out my hand for a shake.

Brittany looks at my hand but doesn't shake it. "But Raphe has his license. You know there's not much to do here. All the kids go into the city sometimes."

The front door chimes, interrupting us as we both turn to see who it is.

I'm saved by the bell and Dylan. When he joins us, his gaze flips back and forth between us. "Am I interrupting something?"

I say, "No," at the same time Brittany says, "Yes."

Brittany lifts her chin and asks Dylan, "Did you and Sawyer ever go into the city when you were dating in high school?"

Dylan's gaze zips to mine. I'm hoping he can read the "please don't answer that question" look in my eyes.

He turns back to Brittany, "I don't have time to chat right now. Do you know where Raphe is? His parents said he never came home after the funeral."

Brittany frowns and grabs her cell. "Let me text him. He usually hits me right back."

"He has more than one phone? I still have his."

Brittany smiles sheepishly. "He got a burner phone until he gets his back. You told him it could be a while, right?"

"Yeah." Dylan crosses his arms. "But I thought you promised Sawyer you wouldn't contact him."

I love that Dylan called Brittany out. It gets old being the bad guy all the time.

Brittany shrugs. "He gave me the new number last night when I was *allowed* to speak with him." She turns to me. "I haven't used it yet."

"Fine. Just text him, please." As her fingers tap, I ask Dylan, "Did Ben talk to Mr. Kingsley? Was Raphe telling the truth about the golf ball?"

Dylan nods. "Kingsley said he's sent you multiple emails you've never returned. He claims he was trying to tell you what happened."

"I didn't even open them. I thought he was trying to contact me about my storefront being out of compliance." I grab my phone and scroll through old mail. "But that doesn't explain the note on the ball."

"At first, Kingsley said he had no idea how something could've been written on the ball. And then he *suddenly* remembered that he did have a ball with some writing on it. Says he was playing golf with his lawyer who wrote something on the ball as a joke. He rummaged through his golf bag but couldn't find it."

"How convenient." I open one of the emails Kingsley sent and scan through it. Sure enough, he explained that a kid had hit a ball through my window by accident. That it shouldn't matter, though, because I was going to have to change out the older window when I remodeled anyway. "Kingsley told the truth about the emails. But what did he claim was written on the ball?"

Dylan pulls out his phone. "Beat by a lawyer. Go home before I bill ya."

I flip through the pictures on my phone until I find the shot I took of the ball. The only words we could make out were Sawyer and go home. But the "S" on Sawyer could be just a crooked "L." It must be hard to write on a dimpled ball.

I hand over my picture of the ball for Dylan to study and say, "He may be telling the truth, I guess. But it doesn't feel like it. The ball wasn't that wet when I took it from Cooper that morning. I think Kingsley made sure he had a plausible alibi. He wants my store to close as much as my uncle does. They'd both like to add a brewpub on the town square, and mine is the only business that isn't doing well."

"I know." Dylan leans against the counter like he's tired. "But without better proof, I can't charge him with anything. Especially because he sent you emails explaining the accident."

"Emails he knew I wouldn't open. It isn't like he couldn't walk fifty feet and find me here at the store to explain what happened."

"Agreed. But if he attempted to scare you away, it didn't work. And Kingsley would be a fool to do anything else now."

I hate to let the guy entirely off the hook. "He should pay for my new window, at least."

"That's what I thought too." Dylan grins and hands me a check. "Can we call it even now and move on?"

The check is for more than the insurance was going to pay. "I'd rather call this 'whoops, I got caught' money, but okay. I'll move on. I hope he and my uncle will stop their games now."

"I let Kingsley know I didn't appreciate threats to my girlfriend."

His girlfriend? It sounds odd to hear that again, but nice at the same time. Not that we don't have a lot of healing to do to get back to where we were before.

Just as I open my mouth to reply, Dylan says, "Hey, by the way. You said something last night about Clint that's been bothering me."

About Clint? Is Dylan still a little jealous? "What did I say?"

"That there was something familiar about him. Did you figure out what it was?"

Oh, that. It was more fun to think Dylan was jealous.

I shake my head. "I can't put my finger on it. Maybe he reminds me of someone I've met before."

Brittany, who'd gone back to tapping keys on the computer, says, "Hey, guys? You need to see this." Her voice shakes like she's afraid.

Dylan circles the counter and leans close to the screen. "What are we looking at?"

Brittany sucks in a big breath. "When Raphe didn't answer, I tracked his cell." She points to the screen and whispers, "That's the funeral parlor. No way he's still there."

"And no way he'd ditch his new phone on his own." Dylan pushes back from the counter. "This is why I didn't want him at the funeral, Sawyer." He heads for the door as he calls for backup.

I should've never let Brittany ask Raphe to come.

Brittany starts to follow, but I grab her arm and stop her. "Hang on. Maybe it's best if we wait here."

Tears bubble in her eyes. "But what if he's hurt?"

Or worse. His name keeps popping up in this investigation. What if the older man Raphe helped was at the funeral and thought Raphe recognized him? "Dylan will take care of Raphe. Can you use those hacker skills and figure out how long that phone hasn't moved? That could be a real help to Dylan."

Brittany nods and pulls herself together. "I'll try."

While she focuses on the computer, I'm trying to hold it together myself. I was the one who allowed her to ask Raphe to attend the funeral.

If anything has happened to Raphe, it's my fault. How will I ever be able to look his poor parents in the eye again? The last thing I'd ever do is put someone in harm's way on purpose. Especially a kid.

CHAPTER 17

*B*rittany and I are sick with unease while waiting to hear news of Raphe from Dylan. We're both at the bookstore, trying to concentrate on our tasks at hand. I'm ordering book inventory, and Brittany's working in the back room on the data from Raphe's phone. I'm still kicking myself for letting Raphe anywhere near that funeral.

My phone rings, busting me out of my musings. "Hey, Madge. What did you find out about Clint?"

"That he got gas the night before he drove here. If he stopped somewhere along the way, he didn't use a credit card to buy anything."

"Too bad." It's probably about a two-hundred-and-thirty-mile trip, so it's possible Clint didn't stop. Me? I drink way too much coffee to make a trip that long without stopping. "I guess we can't verify with certainty when he arrived, then?"

"I didn't say that." Madge chuckles. "I just said he didn't stop to buy anything. This morning, Dylan asked Clint for permission to look into the GPS records on his phone. There's a rush on it, so hopefully, we'll have that information soon. Unless Brittany can find it faster?"

I'm hesitant to ask any more of the kids. Especially until we know if Raphe is okay. "Brittany has her hands full with Raphe's phone. Do you know if they've found him yet?"

"Not yet. Raphe's phone was in the lost and found at the funeral parlor. But no Raphe. Dylan's got everyone looking for him."

My heart aches even worse now. "I think we'll lock up and help. If you hear anything, please let us know."

"Will do." Madge hangs up.

While tucking my phone away, I head to the back to get Brittany. She'll want to help look for Raphe too. I'm relieved Dylan didn't find Raphe bleeding and hurt behind the funeral parlor, but where could the kid be? Maybe he went out to the golf course to practice for the team again. We'll run home and get the car so we can cover more ground.

Brittany is sitting on the floor with her legs crossed and her laptop open. She's so engrossed in whatever she's doing, she doesn't notice me. I sit beside her and give her shoulder a nudge with mine. "What's so interesting?"

Brittany jumps like I startled her. "I found the video of the old man who talked to Raphe in Renee's store. It had been deleted, but I'm better than that. Look."

The screen shows a man, just as Raphe had described

him, chatting and showing Raphe his smartwatch. It's loud enough in the ice cream parlor that we can't hear his voice clearly. "I'm glad to know Raphe wasn't lying about that."

"Yeah. Now I want to watch our video of the book signing. Try to see if I recognize anyone who was at the funeral today. Or if the old man was here in the store too." Brittany taps a few keys and cues up our security footage.

"That's a good idea. Did you have any luck enhancing the sound when Clint whispered something to Angelica?"

Brittany shakes her head. "I couldn't make it clear enough to be sure, but I think he said something like 'it's almost over now.'"

"Which tells us nothing. The reception *was* almost over." I peer harder at the screen. "I started watching this the other day but quit when Dylan told me what happened to Zach's phone." It still freaks me out to see Zach talking and smiling with all the ladies waiting in line hours before his death. "Seems Angelica absently dropped the phone into her purse, thinking it was hers."

"I saw that part the other day and watched it twice. I think it's strange that her phone wasn't charged. She's on it all the time. It doesn't seem right that she'd forget to juice it up."

While we watch the next person shuffle up to the table for Angelica's autograph, I say, "She doesn't have an assistant anymore, remember? Kate probably used to do that for Angelica."

Brittany shrugs. "I guess."

I'm just about to suggest we go help look for Raphe when someone in the video walks through the front door, tugging on the cap on their head. There's a smartwatch on the person's wrist that rings an alarm bell for me. "Can you stop the recording, please?" I lean even closer to the screen to study the slender person wearing jeans, a hoodie, and a baseball cap. "Is that a man or a woman?" I point to the person who now has their back to the camera. The time stamp says it's 3:50 pm.

"It's hard to tell. Why?" Brittany backs up the recording so we can see the person walk into the store again.

"Because Mr. Martinez said he saw Renee go into her store through the back wearing a similar outfit about four o'clock." We watch as the dark-haired person walks through the door again, never looking directly at the camera, as if knowing where the cameras are. By the stride, it's a man. He walks to the far side of the store and picks up a book to browse the back cover, making no attempt to join the others for an autograph. Then he glances over his shoulder, puts the book down, and walks out the door again. All without a clear shot of his face except when he comes through the front door, but then he's wearing sunglasses. Later, he tucks them into the front pocket of the hoodie.

Brittany rewinds the sequence. "Was the line too long, so he left?"

"Maybe." We watch it again. This time, I'm trying to see what he saw when he glanced over his shoulder. "Freeze it there." Zach is talking to a pretty woman in line, and

Angelica is handing a book to a customer. None of the other customers appear to be looking at him. "Can you move it ahead in slow motion from here?"

"Sure." Brittany taps some keys, and the video moves again. She points to the screen. "Does Hoodie Guy nod there? Just a little?"

"Yeah. I saw that too." My heart rate soars as we watch the whole sequence again but in slow motion. Did we just find the murderer? Could that be Clint? He's slender too, has artistic feminine hands, but the hair color is a little off. This person's hair is brown, while Clint's is darker. "Watch Angelica. Did you see that? Is she nodding ever so slightly too? Or is he looking at someone else?" Luckily, my video equipment is brand-new, so the images are pretty clear.

"It's hard to tell. She could be nodding at a fan." Brittany starts the video sequence all over again. "But from behind, that could be a man or a woman. Especially to someone who can't see ten feet in front of him, like Mr. Martinez."

"Exactly what I was thinking. And the hair color is close enough to mistake it for Renee's. Let's ask Mr. Martinez to look at this before we bother Dylan. He's got a lot on his plate right now." And to give him a little time to cool off. He's pretty upset with me.

Brittany slaps the laptop closed and follows me to the front door. I flip over the OPEN sign while she hits the lights.

After I lock up, we walk toward Mr. Martinez's art gallery, and I realize I've forgotten to tell Brittany what

Madge said. "They found Raphe's phone in the lost and found at the funeral home. But they're still looking for him."

"That makes sense." Brittany hurries to catch up with my long strides. "When I watched the video of you tackling Raphe, his phone slid out of his pocket and across the floor. That's what gave me the idea to look at the book-signing video again. I got so caught up that I forgot to tell you about the phone."

"That's okay. I'm glad you thought to look at the footage again. I think we're on to something important."

We arrive at the art gallery, and I tug the door open for Brittany to enter first. "Why don't you fast-forward the video to the point where the guy has his back to the camera before we show Mr. Martinez."

"Sounds good." Brittany heads for the sales counter and opens the laptop.

Mr. Martinez is helping a customer and hasn't even noticed we're here, so I call Dylan to tell him what we found. And because I'm still worried about Raphe. Our little town isn't big enough for someone to be lost in it for long.

Dylan answers with "Just found Raphe. He was at the diner with a reporter."

"Thank goodness." Relief fills me as I slump into a nearby chair. "Was the reporter wearing khaki pants and a rumpled shirt, by chance?"

"Yeah. The same guy who sat next to Kate at the funeral. Says he was asking Raphe questions about what happened at the ice-cream shop before the murder. Kate tipped the reporter off."

"I overheard the reporter on the phone. He said he was looking for another source because it could be sour grapes. Sounds like he was trying to verify something, Kate—the disgruntled employee—told him. My guess is that Kate told the reporter about Angelica's secret."

"Yep. And a lot more." Dylan grunts. "Gotta run."

"Wait. I think we found something important in the book-signing video I'd like to show you."

"You saw the guy in the hat wearing a hoodie?"

"Yes! I think—"

"I saw him too, and I've already shown Mr. Martinez," Dylan barks. Then he pauses for a moment like he's collecting himself. "Mr. Martinez agrees that the person he saw might not have been Renee. So, whatever you're up to now, just stop, Sawyer. You've done enough damage to my case for one day."

I'm still in the doghouse. Probably best not to share that Brittany and I are with Mr. Martinez right now. "Okay. I'll go home now and stay out of things." When I get no response in return, I add, "Want to come over for dinner?"

"Not tonight. I'm busy." He disconnects the call.

Yep. He's officially mad at me.

I never meant to cause trouble. I'm just trying to be helpful. But maybe Dylan's right about me. Perhaps I do try to fix problems I have no business trying to solve. But how does one change their basic nature? And should someone have to do that in order to be with someone else?

Whenever I'm upset, cooking always calms me. I'll go home and make pad thai because Dylan loves that. I'll drop it by his office so he can eat it whenever he has a chance.

Before I can put my phone away, it vibrates again. It's Madge, so I say, "Hi, there. Dylan told me they found Raphe. Any more intel on Clint?" There I go again without even thinking. Dylan just asked me to back off.

Madge says, "Yeah. His GPS showed he got into town after Angelica got bopped, picked her up, and then went to the diner. He couldn't have hit her over the head. And he, assuming he was with his phone, was in San Francisco during the murder."

"Okay, thanks. Talk to you later." I hang up.

Clint's story checks out. Are we back to Kate being the prime suspect? She could have hired the guy in the hoodie to ambush Zach.

Blowing out a long breath in frustration, I join Brittany and fill her in. We pack up the laptop and then slip out the door before Mr. Martinez finishes with his customer.

Once we're on the sidewalk, I say, "I've been thinking about the person in the video. Why would a person wearing a sweatshirt with a hood wear a baseball cap too? Wouldn't it make more sense to just slip the hood on?"

Brittany shakes her head. "If you walk around with the hood pulled up, people freak out. Like you're that unibomber or something."

"It's Unabomber not uni, but I guess that's true. No one thinks twice about a ball cap, though."

"Right. You coming back to the shop?" Brittany asks.

"No. I'm going home. You want to call it a day too?"

"Not yet." Brittany turns toward the bookstore. "I'm still working on how someone hacked Renee's computers. I started a run on the counter computer I'd like to check on. Then I'll head home too."

"Okay. See you in a bit." I turn the opposite way and start up the hill to my house.

I'm trying, but I can't turn off my mind. That guy in the hoodie was probably who Mr. Martinez saw go into Renee's shop. Did the same guy appear in my store during the book signing to be sure Zach was where he was supposed to be? Right before the fake email was sent with the code to the ice-cream shop's back door?

Hoodie Guy would have to beat Zach there to surprise him. But the killer wouldn't want to get there too soon, because what if one of the workers out front needed something from the back? To take that kind of risk meant the killer knew how the ice-cream shop worked. How Renee usually stocks the ice cream right before lunch. If someone had access to the cameras inside the store, they'd be able to study the patterns. Or maybe Raphe, Z, or Annie unwittingly told someone the routine.

The sidewalk under my tired feet turns steep as I climb the hill to my house, but I'm so busy pondering, I barely notice.

I still can't figure who could've hit Angelica over the head. It wasn't Clint. It had to have been someone who didn't know Renee had been locked up. Kate wouldn't know that because Dylan is keeping them separate. And that probably explains why he put Kate at his house in the first place. To isolate her. Will he have to let her go soon? And if so, will Kate go after Angelica again? Dylan said Angelica planned to go home tonight, so maybe he's hoping the San Francisco police will have more resources to protect her.

Shaking my head at all the unknowns still out there, I push all thoughts of murder out of my mind. Instead, I focus on the contents of my pantry. Do I have everything I'll need on hand to make pad thai? I think so, but I might have to substitute cashews for peanuts.

A car's beep sounds behind me, so I stop thinking about food and turn to see who it is.

Gage pulls up next to me in his fancy sports car and opens his passenger door. "Need a lift?"

"Thanks." I climb into the car and shut the door. "Where have you been hiding out? I haven't seen you for days."

"Been trying to avoid you because I know stuff about Renee's case I can't tell you. You're spooky good at tricking people into telling you secrets."

I smile at that. "It's a gift. But I've already made a mess of Renee's case today, so you're safe. I'll keep my superpower to myself. Just this once."

"I appreciate that." Gage puts the car in gear, and we

zoom off. "I was looking for you because I have some news about Brittany's mother."

My stomach drops. "You found her?"

"I did." Gage's expression turns serious. "I'm afraid talking to her is the only way we'll know for sure how she paid for the adoption. And if your uncle had anything to do with it, intending to break the trust."

We pull into my driveway as I ask, "Do you think she'll tell us the truth? She's not known for that."

Gage turns off the car and faces me. "She's hooked up with an older guy who appears to have plenty of money. Maybe just this once, when she isn't desperate, she'll be honest."

"Or maybe because she's settled, she'll regret giving Brittany away and want her back. My mom wouldn't want to see Brittany disappointed when her mom gets itchy feet again. Like she's done so many times in the past." Besides, I have my heart set on seeing Brittany attend a fantastic college and focusing all her smarts in the right direction. To do that, she needs to stick with my family and the trust. Assuming my uncle doesn't mess all that up. "What if we hold off talking to Brittany's mother for now? Keep her in our back pocket if we need her."

"It's your choice." Gage blows out a long breath. "But if we do nothing, and your uncle wins the case, you could lose the house, your bookstore, and the restaurant you want to build."

"Everything I'm trying to save. I owe it to my mom to

try." I close my eyes and lean my head back against the seat. "What have you learned from his lawyers? What are my uncle's chances of winning?"

"There's a clause that's open for interpretation. It could be construed that your mother adopting a child and moving her into the house without advising your uncle could void the terms of the trust. Adding another mouth to feed wasn't what your grandparents wanted to happen."

I open my eyes and roll my head in Gage's direction. "And this is a small town. My uncle could've gotten wind of my mom's intention to adopt Brittany, so he made sure it happened by bankrolling Brittany's mom. Because if my mom had used the trust's money, it'd be a form of notifying my uncle, who reviews all the financial outlays, right?"

"Exactly." Gage's lips thin. "All your mom had to do was tell your uncle her intentions, and then use money from the wine she left you, and all would have been fine because she wouldn't have used any trust money. It could be argued that your mother supported Brittany with funds from the trust, thereby voiding the terms. That clause was in there because of your father. No offense."

"None taken." My grandparents didn't want my mother supporting my father. I get that. If only my grandparents had lived long enough to see that my dad isn't a bad guy; he just isn't the best magician. While he's always broke, he has a big heart, and he truly loved my mom. And my mom always loved him.

But I don't want to see Brittany hurt any further by her mom. "Can we keep Brittany out of this?"

"We can try." Gage takes off his glasses and cleans them on his shirt. Once the glasses are back in place, he says, "I'd like to talk to Brittany's mother in person. Which means a trip to LA. But I can't go until this mess with Renee is settled."

"If it takes too long, maybe I'll go to LA." I open my car door and step out. "Hopefully, Dylan can solve this case before my uncle's lawyers file their petitions. Thanks, Gage."

"No problem." He starts the car and waves as he calls out, "I'll keep you up to date."

I return the wave and wait until he's turned the corner before I head up the front porch of my house. Cooper has heard me and is barking happily inside. I could use a cuddle from my pooch right about now.

After I open the door, Cooper bounds out to greet me on the front porch. I sink to the top step and pet him as I contemplate my life.

If I lose everything, I'd let my mom down. On the other hand, my sister has always told me it isn't worth the battle with my uncle. Just let him have it all and move on. Be happy. Go to France and work under a great chef like I'd thought about doing last year before I learned Mom was sick.

But now I have Brittany, who I genuinely care for, and Dylan, who'd had a whole lot more going on than I'd known about when he broke up with me. He was letting me go that day at the church in case he ended up in jail for his father's sins. Even better, my dad and my sister's family are nearby. I've missed them.

I have the wine my mom left too. Not worth enough to open a restaurant, but enough to get a new start for Brittany and me.

Despite my uncle, and if I do lose everything, I have a right to live in Sunset Cove if I want to. After being away for so long, I've realized it's not such a bad place. Small, yes. Filled with the nosiest bunch ever? True. But it's also filled with people who truly know me and who care about me. Something I've never found anywhere else.

As I pull my little teddy-bear-like dog closer, I whisper, "I'm not sure how yet, but we're going to beat Uncle Frank at his own game, right, Cooper?"

Cooper, who I swear understands every word I speak to him, woofs his approval.

Maybe Cooper *does* understand me. My mom insisted we all have multiple lives. She used to say she'd love to come back as a dog because all they have to do is love their owners, eat, and sleep.

Mom purchased Cooper for me before she died, and before he was born. Maybe she hoped one could choose whose dog to be in the afterlife?

I stare into Cooper's eyes. "Are you in there, Mom?"

Cooper winks, totally freaking me out.

No. Dogs wink sometimes, don't they? I'll have to look

that up on the internet. "Come on, whoever you are. Let's go see about dinner."

Cooper races me to the open door, probably hoping it's time for *his* dinner, and we head for the kitchen. I start pulling what I'll need from the pantry when my cell rings. I'm tempted to ignore it, but guilt that it could be important makes me look.

It's Brittany. "Hey. What's up?"

"Remember that computer run I was waiting on? I found the original IP address for the person who hacked Renee's computers. It's one I recognized immediately once I followed the breadcrumbs all over the world and back."

"Finally." Hope surges inside. "Whose is it?"

Brittany whispers, "Yours."

CHAPTER 18

I'm heating up my wok as my blood sizzles to an even higher temperature. How could my computer have been used to hack Renee's? It makes no sense. The only thing that makes perfect sense is that someone is diverting attention to others while they get away with murder, just like my dad said. It's annoying.

A smirking Brittany joins me in the kitchen and slips onto a stool at the island. "How long do you think it'll be before your boyfriend arrests you for hacking?"

"He's barely speaking to me as it is. This isn't going to help." I give the chicken a quick stir. "You need to call him and tell him what you found."

"Why?" Brittany's forehead crumples. "Let the grump figure it out on his own. I mean, it's obvious you didn't do it.

I'm still working on who did. When I figure it out, that's when I'll call him."

"I'd rather tell him first. Before the evidence lab finds out." I turn and smash the cashews with more force than is required. I'm angry and feeling violated that someone has accessed my electronics too. The poor cashews are paying the price.

When the doorbell rings, Brittany smiles. "Whoops. Too late. He's here to haul you off in cuffs."

"Dylan wouldn't ring the bell. He'd come to the back like he always does." I crack the eggs into the side of the wok and then add soy sauce before I head for the door with Cooper on my heels.

Brittany says, "Maybe he's ringing the bell because he's here on official business. To arrest you!"

I call out, "Stir the dinner, please, smart-mouth."

I wipe my hands on my apron and open the door. Clint and Angelica, still dressed in the clothes they wore to the funeral, are standing on my porch. Clint has a big box in his arms.

I open the screen door. "Hi, guys. I thought you'd already be on your way to San Francisco."

Angelica points at the box. "When I was packing the car, I found another box of books in the trunk. My publisher provides copies for events like yours, so I thought you'd like to have them. Sell them, give them away, or maybe give copies to your book club. It's up to you."

"Thanks. That's so nice of you." I step back so Clint can bring the box inside.

"It's nothing. Really." Angelica follows Clint inside too. "What smells so good?"

"I'm making pad thai. There's plenty. Would you like to join us?" I close the door behind them and hold my hand out toward the bench that sits by the door. "You can put the books there, Clint."

"We'd love to stay." Angelica tosses her designer purse on the bench right next to the box. "We're starving but couldn't bear another greasy burger from the diner or another of my mother's casseroles. We were going to wait until we got to the city to eat."

Clint nods. "It smells amazing. Thanks, Sawyer."

"It's the least I can do." I lead the way down the hall. "You've both had a difficult day. I'm so sorry I made it worse with my disruption at the service."

Angelica sighs. "You tackling that boy actually gave us the excuse we needed to leave. I'd had enough with the former girlfriends."

"I can imagine." I poke the swinging door and hold it open for them to pass by. Maybe this is an excellent opportunity to learn what they know about the case. And lips are always looser with alcohol. "Would you like some wine?"

Clint smiles. "That'd be great." He sees Brittany and says, "Hi, there."

Brittany lifts a hand. "Hi again. I'll get the glasses, Sawyer."

"Thanks." I check on the dinner. Brittany has added the noodles, and she even stirred in siracha for some kick. I grab a pair of chopsticks and take a sample. "Brittany has outdone herself. Please have a seat." I add the sliced green onions and sprinkle cashews on the top.

Brittany sets the wineglasses on the island and then grabs two more bowls. "I just babysat it. Sawyer's the chef, not me."

"It was a combined effort." As I pour out the wine, a muffled thump sounds from the hallway. I swivel my head in search of the likely culprit. Sure enough, Cooper is nowhere to be found. After the adults all take a sip, I set my glass down. "I'll be right back. I need to check on something."

I quickly head for the entry. My dog is the nosiest little creature on earth. I'm hoping Angelica didn't leave her purse open. Cooper is known to snoop for mints and gum if given the opportunity.

"What are you doing, sir?" I place my hands on my hips and wait for Cooper to extract his furry face from Angelica's purse that's now on the floor.

He gives me a doggy grin and an innocent tail wag like he's glad to see me.

"Bad dog!" I whisper and lean down to scoop up the things that have fallen out. Just as I'm zipping the purse and placing it back on the bench, something shiny by Cooper's paw catches my attention. It's the locket Zach gave Renee senior year in high school. Could Zach have given an identical one to Angelica?

After glancing over my shoulder to be sure I'm alone, I

pry the little heart open with my fingernail. Inside, younger versions of Renee and Zach stare back at me. And the clasp is still broken. I was there when Renee ripped the locket from around her neck in anger many years ago, breaking it.

This makes no sense. Why would Angelica have it?

A thought hits like a hammer to the gut. Angelica was in Renee's bedroom when I found her on the floor. Was Angelica stealing the locket? And who made the fake call to her mother's house asking Angelica to meet Renee there?

Could Angelica have gotten there first and decided to snoop in Renee's jewelry box? Was it a jealousy thing?

I'm so confused, but there's no way I'm letting Angelica take Renee's locket, so I slip it into my pocket and replace the purse on the bench. "Good boy, Cooper." I give him a pat and hurry back to the kitchen. My phone is on the island. I need to sneak a text to Dylan, confessing to my crime. But then, is it a crime to steal back stolen property? I guess I'll find out.

When I get back to the kitchen, Brittany has dished up everyone's bowls, so I join our guests at the island. But I can't find my phone. I know I set it on the granite after I talked to Brittany earlier because I was cooking dinner when she called.

Did Brittany move it? No, the island is massive. There wouldn't be any reason for her to touch my phone.

Brittany is making small talk as I stuff spicy noodles into my mouth. My eyes continue their reconnaissance mission around the kitchen, but the phone is nowhere to be found.

My gut's suddenly uneasy, but not from the spicy

noodles. I'd put my phone down where I always do. Brittany has never touched it before. Add in the stolen locket, and now I have a feeling something's up.

I try to tune in to the conversation, but the alarm going off in my head is making it hard to concentrate.

Clint who's seated to my right, reaches for his wineglass as he and Brittany discuss their favorite crime novel. Luckily, Brittany knows a lot about books, unlike me. I'm still learning.

My mind races, trying to think of an excuse to leave the table and find a way to send Dylan a message when Clint's suit cuff slides up and exposes a smartwatch. Just like the one Renee had. But it's Clint's unusual feminine hands that are sending shivers up my spine. I've seen them before. Not only at the diner when I first met him. Sometime before that. But I can't remember where. Has he been in my store before?

As Brittany continues to debate the inaccuracies in a recent bestseller with Clint and Angelica, I'm officially worried. The guy in the hoodie who came into my store seemed to know where the cameras were. What if it was Clint in the hoodie? He has the slender build and a smartwatch. Had Clint scouted out my store in advance? But if that were true, wouldn't I have recognized his handsome features when I met him at the diner? I just can't be sure. I was so incredibly wrong about Raphe. Maybe my instincts are off.

Either way, I want to move these two along and out of my house so I can tell Dylan about the stolen necklace. "I'm sorry I don't have anything to offer for dessert. I'd have made something special had I known you'd be joining us."

"No problem." Angelica sets her wineglass down and turns to me. "That was an amazing dinner, thank you. We need to get going, but I'd really like to hear what you know about Zach's death, Sawyer. Dylan has been very tight-lipped the last day or so. You must have some good pillow talk."

Oh. So maybe that's why they're really here.

I shake my head as I finish my wine. "Dylan and I are still trying to figure out what our new relationship will be, so no pillow talk." I probably shouldn't mention the part about Dylan asking me to stay out of the investigation. I don't want to appear to be gathering intel on my own.

Clint narrows his eyes and growls, "But you must've asked. I understand Renee is your best friend."

"She is." Adrenaline is pulsing through my veins, so I fold my hands to steady them. "But I trust Dylan will get to the bottom of things." I glance at Angelica to see if she's upset by Clint's anger too. But she doesn't seem fazed.

"I see." Clint's expression turns dark. "On second thought, maybe we should spring for dessert before we go, Angelica. Especially because we crashed the party." He plasters on a smile. "Brittany? Would you mind running to the store for a cake? Chocolate would be nice." Clint stands and grabs money from his wallet. "And if they have ice cream, get that as well."

Brittany holds up a finger. "We actually have a few

dessert options here." She hops off her stool and grabs the cookie jar. "I made these the other day."

Clint lays his hand on my arm. "While I'm sure those are amazing, a meal like we just had deserves cake, am I right, Sawyer?"

At first, his hand on my arm seems friendly, until his grip tightens.

His eyes dare me to argue as he squeezes harder. Clint wants information from me. And he's trying to get rid of Brittany, so I need to let him. I can't allow Brittany to be dragged into whatever this is. It feels dangerous.

Angelica's still calm, though, so maybe I'm overreacting.

Forcing a smile at Brittany, I say, "Yeah. Cake sounds great. Why don't you take Cooper too? He needs a walk."

Clint's grip relaxes slightly, but I'm still trying not to grimace. I need Brittany to be well away from whatever Clint has in mind. Just in case.

Cooper must realize I'm afraid, because he chooses that moment to be a fierce guard dog instead of a teddy bear. He growls at Clint and lunges at his leg.

Brittany says, "Cooper? What are you doing?" She reaches down and scoops up our pooch.

Fear makes it hard to get enough air, but I manage, "Sorry, Clint. He's only done that once before. Brittany, can you take him along, please?"

Brittany, clearly confused by Clint's dessert request and Cooper's behavior, locks eyes with me. I'm hoping she remembers the only other time Cooper got upset—with Wade, the guy who tried to kill me.

Brittany slowly nods like she understands, but I can't be sure. She says, "I'll take Cooper with me. Be right back." She turns and hurries out of the kitchen.

Thank goodness, Brittany's safe.

Once the front door slams shut, Clint tugs me to my feet. "I hear you and your little book club have been busy. And it was your IP address used to hack Renee's accounts. Time to spill, Sawyer." He finally releases my arm.

How would he know what Brittany found unless he's the real hacker? Or Brittany told Raphe about my IP address before she told me.

As I rub the soreness away, I'm trying to think and breathe at the same time. Neither function is working as it should. "I… don't know what you're talking about." I glance at Angelica, who's pouring herself another glass of wine. "Really." Lying is probably forgivable when attempting to save one's life.

Angelica takes a long sip from her glass before she says, "Please excuse Clint's frustration, Sawyer. Dylan is a nice guy, but this is a small town without the resources a larger city would have. We're worried he'll let whoever killed Zach get away."

Angelica is perfectly calm, but Clint is barely controlling his temper. It's confusing. But one thing's for sure now, Clint has underlying rage inside that could make him a killer.

I stammer, "Dylan won't rest until the murderer is found.

I can promise you that." There's a block of knives on the counter by the stove. Maybe if I can slowly slip over there, I can grab one. Just in case.

Clint leans closer. "Where's Renee? And what's to keep her from sneaking over the border some night?" Clint points a long finger at me. "Or for you to help her?"

I take a step back and closer to the knives. "Renee didn't kill Zach."

"Is that what Dylan thinks?" Angelica stands and moves beside Clint. "Or is that what you want to believe?"

"It's what *I know*. It's what *everyone* here knows. It's obvious someone has set her up. It's just a matter of time before Dylan figures out who the real murderer is."

Clint locks eyes with Angelica. "Maybe she's right. The hometown element was overlooked in an otherwise perfect crime."

Angelica's eyes narrow. "So maybe we make sure the only one in town capable of solving the murder is so distraught, he can't think straight." Angelica moves toward the knives. "Perhaps we should do away with the one thing Dylan has always loved?"

Oh, no. Angelica is in on this too?

Clint's expression turns stone cold. "Yes. And we can use the necklace to make Dylan think Renee did it."

My heart is beating so hard, I can't think straight. All I know is that I need to run!

I start for the back door, but Clint is faster.

He snakes an arm around my waist and slams me against

the pantry door, trapping my arms behind me. His free hand tightens around my neck, making it hard to breathe. "You're not going anywhere, Sawyer. We need you to be the black moment in our hero's journey. I'm afraid you know a little too much, so this story isn't going to have a happy ending, is it, Angelica?" As he glances at Angelica his grip lightens slightly on my neck so I can breathe again.

"Sadly, no." Angelica makes a tsking noise. "Clint said you were no computer expert after his sales visit to your store. But clearly, you were lying to him."

Sales visit? The only sales visit I've had— *That's* where I'd seen Clint's hands before. He came into my store to try to sell me a machine that prints books on demand. He'd tested my internet and stolen my IP address. "You were wearing a disguise, obviously," I croak out as best I can.

Clint's right brow arches. "Or am I wearing one now? You'll never know, will you?"

"Were you the 'old man' who tricked Raphe into changing Renee's watch data too?" It's hard to get enough air to speak.

Clint smiles. "You have been a busy little investigator, haven't you?"

Angelica calls out, "Oooh. Maybe this would be a better way?"

I'd recognize the swish of one of my extremely sharp knives being extracted from the block anywhere. I need to get away, but Clint has pressed his whole body against mine. His thumb pressing into the middle of my throat is cutting off my air supply again.

Please let Brittany have gone for help.

Angelica holds my sharpest chef's knife as she glances at Clint. "It'd be perfectly ironic if the chef is killed by one of her own knives, wouldn't it?"

He lets go of my neck and accepts the knife from Angelica. "Especially if we make it look like Renee's gone nuts and killed Sawyer too." Clint's face lights with a sick grin. "It'd require a little tweaking of the storyline, but it'd be the perfect ending for chapter twenty. Renee's necklace at the scene will seal the deal for the sheriff."

Things are starting to make more sense, so I draw a deep breath and ask, "I just happened to catch you sneaking around in Renee's bedroom, didn't I, Angelica? You sent that recording to your mom in case you got caught, giving you a reason to be at Renee's house." No wonder the doc sent her home. Angelica never got hit over the head.

Angelica ignores my question and squeals with delight. "Dylan will be so distraught, he'll throw Renee in jail forever. We've made sure he has all the evidence he'd need to convince a jury. This is the perfect twist, babe. We'll have a bestseller for sure. Maybe another movie deal."

I can't believe what I'm hearing. These two are writing a murder mystery, and I'm going to be added to the body count.

Angelica turns her attention to me. "You know what they say, Sawyer. Curiosity kills the cat. If only you'd minded your own business, Kate, the husband stealer, would've been arrested for framing Renee and killing Zach.

All would have ended the way it should, and Clint and I would have our own happily ever after. Too bad you won't be able to learn from this life lesson, because you'll be dead."

Dead?

Black dots dance in front of my eyes. But I can't pass out. I have to buy some time to figure a way out of this. "So it won't hurt to tell me how you did it, will it?" I'm banking on Angelica's big ego to make her talk.

"Still curious? Even when you're about to die? Shall we tell her, darling?" Angelica runs a hand through Clint's mussed hair to fix it. "Or just put Renee's little lapdog out of her misery?"

Panicked, I blurt, "How'd you make it look like I hacked Renee? When clearly, you hacked her information." My voice sounds deep and raspy from my nearly crushed windpipe. Like it's not even mine.

Clint raises a brow. "First, tell me how an amateur like you figured that out. I can't have plot holes in the story."

I have no idea how Brittany figured that out. "You left a footprint behind." I overheard Brittany say that once. I hope it makes sense.

"Really?" Clint pushes the knife tip under my chin. "Tell me more."

That's about the extent of my computer hacking knowledge. What did Brittany just say a few minutes ago? It's incredibly hard to put a sentence together with a knife at my throat. "I had to chase all over the world and back. But I found you." No way can I let them know Brittany is the brains here. I have to keep her safe.

Clint presses the knife harder against my skin as warmth trickles down my neck. "Found me where?"

Angelica says, "Just do it, Clint. That kid'll be back any minute."

My neck throbs, but I'm desperate to keep Clint talking to buy myself time. "The necklace Zach gave Renee will never work, by the way. Renee never wore it after the breakup. Dylan will see right through that clue."

Clint lets up some of the pressure on the knife. Thankfully. "How do you know about the necklace?"

Angelica hisses, "She must've been snooping in my purse. But she's stalling, Clint. Let's get this over with so we can go."

He presses the knife against my neck again, even harder. "Thank you, Sawyer. We'll use the scarf Angelica took to plant in Kate's apartment instead. And thanks again for the incredible meal. You're a talented chef. It's a shame I have to kill you."

This is it. The end.

I close my eyes and try not to whimper from the pain as I wait for my life to pass before my eyes. But thoughts of who will take care of Brittany and what will happen to Dylan, my family, and Cooper when I die all echo in my head.

A sharp crack like splintering wood sounds before Dylan's voice shouts, "Police. Drop your weapon!"

Clint releases me, and my knees give out. I land with a

thump on my rear as Clint whispers to Angelica, "Send the text."

Angelica nods and taps something on her phone while Clint lunges at Dylan.

I should probably try to help Dylan by containing Angelica, but I'm feeling kind of dizzy. When I look down, it's obvious why I'm so light-headed. I'm covered in blood. I hate the sight of blood, just like my father does. I want to be sick, but that'd make a bigger mess in my kitchen. I hate a messy kitchen.

That I'm thinking about my kitchen makes no sense. I should help Dylan.

When I gather the strength to lift my head again, Angelica is gone.

Foggy confusion takes over my brain as I watch everything play out before me. Dylan is wrestling the knife away from Clint. After it skids across my kitchen floor, fists start flying. Finally, Dylan throws Clint to the floor like a rag doll and body-slams him.

Dylan shoves his knee into Clint's back and contains him, while glancing my way, concern etched on his face.

Those little black dots are back again, though, and all I can think is, *Stick that ending in your stupid book, Clint and Angelica,* before everything goes black.

CHAPTER 19

My eyelids must be superglued together. As hard as I try, I can't seem to pry them open. I'd really like to confirm I'm still alive.

What I do know is that my right hand is toasty warm, settled into a big rough one that I hope is Dylan's, and my left is cradled in a warm smaller one.

Antiseptic hangs heavy in the air. Luckily, I doubt that's how the afterlife smells. I hope I'm in our tiny hospital/clinic.

I try one more time to open my eyes, and this time I get little slits to form. The room is dim, like it's nighttime, and the back of my hand is hooked up to an IV. Dylan's head is on the hospital mattress next to our entangled fingers. I'd forgotten how cute he is when he's sleeping.

I swivel my head to see who's holding my other hand, and

my neck screams in pain. Brittany has assumed the same position as Dylan. Neither of them can be comfortable, but I love that they have both stuck by my side. I'd have done exactly the same for them.

Not wanting to wake them, I close my eyes again, but now I can't sleep. Images of what happened in my kitchen assault my brain. I don't want to think about that ever again.

"Sawyer?" Dylan's voice whispers in my ear. "Can you hear me?"

A light squeeze on my hand encourages me to force my eyes open again. This time, I can open them all the way. The room is still dim, but light fills the shaded windows like it's morning. I must've fallen asleep again last night.

Dylan's face, complete with morning stubble, is right next to mine. "Don't try to talk. Just blink if you can hear me."

Instead, I smile because I'm elated to see him. I wasn't sure I ever would again.

"Welcome back." His pretty blue eyes go all misty.

Dylan's tears make my eyes water too.

He clears his throat. "Your sister will be here soon. She's been bossing these docs around."

My sister, Megan, the fancy brain surgeon, is always busy, but rarely bossy. She must be worried about me.

But wait. Dylan said welcome back? How long have I been asleep? I open my mouth to ask.

"Nope." Dylan lays a finger over my lips to stop me. "Zero speaking. Those are the rules. Just for a few days."

A few days? But I have so many questions.

271

"Here." Dylan shakes his head as he pulls his phone from his uniform shirt pocket. "Good thing you're not one of those nuns vowed to silence. You'd get kicked out the first ten minutes."

I chuckle as I accept the phone, but stop because it hurts my throat. I pull up his note app and type, *Are Clint and Angelica in jail? And are Renee and Kate safe?* I hand the phone back.

Brittany has woken up now and joins us on Dylan's side of the bed. "Hey. 'Bout time you woke up, you lazy bum." Brittany gently hugs me.

After she releases me, I grab her hand and give it a reassuring squeeze while we wait for Dylan to read my note.

He says, "Clint and Angelica are in jail, but they lawyered up and aren't talking. Renee and Kate are staying put until I can figure out if they're safe. I don't know if Clint and Angelica have a partner still out there."

Brittany says, "What about Sawyer? She's a sitting duck in here."

Dylan takes my free hand, "You'll have an armed deputy outside your room twenty-four seven until we can figure things out."

I nod but then impatiently pull my hand from his and signal I want the phone back. I quickly type all the things Clint confessed while trying to off me. Brittany and Dylan both lean over the bed and read along as I type.

Brittany says, "Wow. They were actually making you a character in their book while they tried to kill you?"

I nod and type as fast as I can, *They said they'd planned the perfect murder, but Clint said he couldn't have holes in the plot. Find the manuscript! All the details will probably be in it until chapter twenty, when they changed things up!*

Dylan shakes his head. "The San Francisco police seized all their electronics. Said all the hard drives had been wiped."

Wiped? How could that be? They must have backups of the books they write together. But then, they couldn't leave evidence of all the hacking they did either.

I stew over this for a moment and then go over what happened in my kitchen step by step. Looking for clues I might have forgotten to tell Dylan. I type, *Clint told Angelica to send a text just as you busted through my back door. Could she have been wiping the data somehow?*

Brittany says, "Yep. They must've planned that in case they got caught. That's pretty sophisticated stuff. We might need Raphe's dad for help with this one. He's the best programmer around." Brittany turns to Dylan. "That is if you say he can help."

Dylan frowns. "If he's the best, maybe Raphe's father is working for Clint and Angelica. Raphe accessed Renee's computers from their home. It'd be like an open door to pull all this off."

Brittany's eyes go wide. "His dad lost almost everything when a hacker stole their game data. Could he be desperate enough to do that? And to involve his own kid?"

"Desperate people do despicable things. We don't know

who we can trust yet. So not a word about this to anyone, Brittany. You understand?"

She nods. "I get it."

He says, "I need to go talk to the SFPD. Let's hope the good guys are as proficient at tech as the bad guys." Dylan leans down and gives me a kiss. "I'll be back to check on you as soon as I can. Promise you'll get some rest? And no talking. Megan's already threatened to gag you." He winks at me.

I smile and then make a cross over my heart. It hurts to laugh, much less talk, anyway. Knowing my sister, she probably told the docs to drug me up for a day because it'd be impossible for me to keep quiet otherwise. Actually, I can't even be mad about that, if it's true. It hurts to swallow too.

After Dylan leaves, Brittany pulls out my phone and hands it to me. "Found this in the junk drawer in the island last night. Either your mind is going like Annie's, or our dinner guests hid it the day before yesterday."

The day before yesterday? Have I been asleep that long? Right now, the details since I was almost killed feel as foggy as Charlie said Annie's memory gets sometimes.

Wait a minute. Maybe Annie can save us! I open my note app and type, *Annie told me she gets all of Angelica's stories early,* then I stick my phone under Brittany's nose.

Brittany reads my note and then sits on the side of the bed. "Maybe she's already read this one and could tell us all about it?" She slides closer to me so we can stop handing the phone back and forth and just read it. "That is if we can rely on her memory."

Exactly.

I type, *Annie said she gets the first half of the story to give initial impressions. Then she makes comments and sends it back. They send her the completed manuscript later. But the words disappear off her hard drive after thirty days. Maybe we're not too late. Dylan confiscated her laptop. Let's go!* Brittany hops up, and I throw my covers back.

I'm just about to jump out of bed when my sister's voice calls out, "Stop right there!" Megan, who got my dad's dark hair and startling blue eyes, slams her hands on her hips. She's pretty laid-back most of the time, so she means business.

Darn it. Why couldn't we have figured this out five minutes earlier? But then, I'm not sure what I would've done with my IV. Rolling it along wouldn't have worked.

I tuck my legs under the sheets again and then start typing on my note app, explaining I feel fine, and please unhook me from the IV. Then I shove the phone her way.

My sister reads the note and shakes her head. "You feel fine because your IV is filled with happy drugs. You're welcome for that, by the way." She hands the phone back and then hugs me. "You could've died, Sawyer. I wish you'd quit finding trouble. It's all you've done since you moved back home."

I type, *Sorry. Am I ever going to speak again?*

"Unfortunately, yes." My sister's grin turns mischievous.

I swat Megan's arm and roll my eyes.

Meg leans closer. "But seriously, we had to fix minor

fractures in the cartilage of your larynx from being choked that need to heal, along with your stitches. Both your body and your voice need rest."

I nod and then type a note to Brittany. *Will you call Madge and tell her we need a peek at Annie's laptop? Tell her we'd ask Dylan, but he's on his way to the city.* I hand the phone back to Brittany.

My sister reads the screen over Brittany's shoulder and sighs. "Only if you promise to rest, Sawyer, while Brittany figures this out. Seriously."

I nod as much as my aching neck will allow, and type. *Promise.*

Megan calls up my chart on the computer and taps a few keys, and then she messes around with my IV before she turns to Brittany. "Go ahead. Call Madge." Then Meg points at me. "You're going to let the computer expert here handle this, right?"

I lift my chin in affirmation before I lean back against the pillows and close my eyes. I'm really tired all of a sudden. Brittany can handle it from here. Assuming we're in time to retrieve the story.

Someone tucks my sheets over me, so I crack open an eye.

Meg whispers, "I added something to your IV to make you sleep because you can't be trusted. Lance and the kids want to visit after work. Dad's on his way too, from some state fair. We'll all see you later. Sweet dreams. Love you."

I mouth, *Love you too,* and then allow sleep to claim me.

A WEEK LATER, the book club is about to convene in my bookstore. This time, we have plenty to talk about for a change. It's the first time I've been allowed to step foot in my store since the "incident" with Clint and Angelica trying to kill me. Brittany has been handling everything for me. And doing a fantastic job.

The good news is, my voice sort of came back this morning. It's gravelly still, and I can only use it sparingly, but I'm eager to hear all the details I've missed while trapped at home, recovering per my sister's strict orders. I wasn't allowed visitors because it'd be too tempting to speak. It was only Cooper and me every day. Dylan and Brittany wouldn't tell me a thing about Zach's case, so that's why I'm here. To finally get some answers.

And now that I can speak, I'm going to give Dylan a piece of my mind when we're alone about holding me prisoner, but for now, Brittany is going to get my wrath. The kid has been avoiding me because she's smart.

I find Brittany behind the counter, closing out the register for the day, so I whisper, "I'm mad at you." It's hard to sound stern when whispering.

"I know." Brittany smiles. "But Meg and Dylan gave me strict orders to keep you out of the loop. And I'm more afraid of them than you."

Great. Some surrogate mother I make.

Before I can think of a good comeback, Madge comes

rushing in the front door, followed by the Admiral, Julie, and Nick. They all stop and pet Cooper and then settle into chairs in the small kitchen area. I join them and arrange the croissants on the pretty platters my mom always used. Then I pull mugs out for the vanilla roast that's calling my name. Not that I'd ever admit it to this crowd, but I'm tired. Recovery has been too slow for my liking, and it's been kicking me in the rear end.

After everyone has their carbs and caffeine, I croak out, "Looks like we're all here. Madge, fill us in, please." Cooper sits by me and lays a paw on my leg, reminding me to pet him.

As I indulge my dog's whims, the bell at the front door sounds, and we all crane our necks to see who it is. Dylan, dressed in street clothes, pulls up a chair and sits next to me. My traitorous dog abandons me and joins Dylan.

He grins, "Figured I might be able to fill in a few details too. Unless you're still mad at me?"

I'm not really mad at him. Just annoyed. I know it's not his fault he couldn't keep me in the loop. My sister was probably the real gatekeeper.

But Dylan could've spilled a few details, couldn't he?

I cross my arms. "You can stay. But you're walking me home later so I can give you a piece of my mind in private."

Madge chuckles and then clears her throat. Just as she's about to begin, Renee and Gage show up and join us as well. That Renee isn't in hiding anymore must mean things are good again.

"Sorry we're late." Renee gives me a quick hug, and then she and Gage settle on the other side of me. Brittany slips her rump on the counter by the sink and is busy with her phone, pretending to look bored, so all is right in the world again.

Madge grins. "Sawyer, you saved the day. Annie's computer had the first half of the book Angelica and Clint were working on."

The Admiral raises a finger. "Luckily, as we all know, the first half sets up most stories, so we had all the details we needed to solve the crime. The names and professions of the characters were changed, though, of course."

I shake my head. "Wouldn't they be afraid someone would read the book and see how close the story resembled what happened to Zach?"

Brittany joins in, "That's the interesting part. Because in their story, the bad guy has to be caught and brought to justice. Whereas Clint and Angelica never intended to be caught, so the second half of the book is where they intended to solve the crime, and it's a red herring as far as what really happened."

Julie frowns. "I'm confused."

Nick nods. "Yeah, me too. Start from the beginning, Madge."

Madge puffs up like a proud peacock in her bright red Christmas sweater with what looks like an elf on the front. Or it could be a snowman. Hard to tell.

Madge says, "Okay, this is a little like something Sawyer's

dad would do. Make everyone look one way, while Clint and Angelica pull off the crime. Also, it's important to note that this book wouldn't have come out for more than a year after this crime. By then, everyone was supposed to have believed Kate found out Zach had been texting Renee again, got jealous, killed Zach, and then set Renee up to take the fall. Simple. And nothing like the hacking story Angelica and Clint were writing with the help of Raphe's father, who'd become a victim of a similar crime. But were the stories really so different?"

Julie says, "They don't sound anything alike."

Madge nods. "That was the point, but upon closer scrutiny, and with help from Raphe's dad and Kate, Dylan was able to find hacking parallels between how Renee and Kate were set up and with the details in the book."

Dylan nods. "Clint and Angelica heard about the ransom crime against Raphe's father's company. He'd studied the crime and taken steps to protect his company from further intrusions. Clint and Angelica hired him to teach them how to use the same techniques to make their story realistic but were, in fact, using him to plan their own crime. Except Angelica and Clint made one mistake. They forgot about the human factor."

Nick asks, "What human factor?"

"Me." Dylan pauses for a sip of my coffee. "I've known Renee all my life. She'd never harm Zach. And my gut told me Kate wasn't guilty either. But even more telling, Angelica kept asking the wrong questions when I interviewed her. She was far too interested in the small details of the case as opposed to being focused on finding the murderer, as most grieving spouses would. Because obviously, she already knew Clint had killed Zach. I recognized this behavior from personal experience from my past." Dylan locks eyes with me as he hands my warm cup back.

He's talking about his father. His dad knew he'd driven his mother to her death and had tried to cover it up.

I ask, "Then why use Raphe? Why did Clint dress up as an old man to get Raphe to change the smartwatch data?"

Dylan starts to answer, but Madge can't stand being left out, so she blurts, "Because the smartwatch and its data weren't in the manuscript. Clint and Angelica didn't want Raphe's dad to question anything."

The Admiral asks, "Then what was going on with Kate and the reporter? Was she going to spill the ghostwriting secret?"

Dylan shakes his head. "When Angelica found out about Zach's affair with Kate, and he'd told her he was leaving, Angelica told him that his timing was perfect. Because after so many years of writing mysteries, she and Clint had finally figured out how to pull off the perfect crime. She said the book would be a bestseller, and she'd be glad she wouldn't have to share any of the money with him."

Madge adds, "At first, Zach took her at her word, but then when odd things happened to his and Kate's bank accounts, he got scared and told Kate he feared that he was going to be the victim of Angelica and Clint's perfect crime.

Kate wanted that story out there after Zach turned up dead."

I'm still confused about something. "Why use my IP address in this whole mess? It makes no sense."

Brittany says, "That's exactly why. It makes no sense because you had nothing to do with Zach or Angelica. It was a false rabbit hole for the cops to follow. Raphe and his dad showed the cops what really happened after they figured out their role in the crime. Raphe and his father never meant to harm anyone. With their help, the evidence will put Angelica and Clint away for the rest of their lives."

I'm still absorbing everything when Madge says, "So two mystery crime writers became so full of themselves, they became delusional, thinking they could pull off the perfect whodunnit. And they were willing to risk their freedom to prove it. That's just sad, isn't it?"

Dylan says, "Yes, but it would have been sadder if Brittany hadn't tripped something online that alerted Clint that their plan wasn't as perfect as he'd thought. They would've executed their plan, causing a jury to send an innocent person to jail. And if Brittany hadn't picked up on Sawyer's distress in the kitchen that day and run for help, Angelica and Clint might've gotten away with their perfect crime." Dylan takes my hand. "I'd say we owe a lot to you guys, and especially Sawyer and Brittany for being ..."

I fill in the blank, "Nosy, obnoxious, and stubborn?"

Dylan laughs. "Yes. All those things, but even better, tenacious about seeing justice served for those you love."

Renee says, "A toast is in order. Thanks, you guys." She lifts her mug, and everyone else does the same. "Here's to the best mystery book club ever!"

As they all toast each other, Dylan squeezes my hand. "Let Brittany close up so I can walk you home. I want to get my lecture over with."

I glance over my shoulder and find Brittany. "Okay if I go?" Brittany has proven she can run the store by herself, but maybe she's tired of it and I need to stay.

Brittany gives me a thumbs-up and goes back to chatting with Madge.

"I guess I can go." Once we're outside on main street, a furry body brushes by my leg. Cooper hasn't let me out of his sight since Clint hurt me. "Can you walk like a good boy without your leash?"

Cooper wags his tail and prances up the hill toward my house. "I guess that's another yes." I let out a long sigh. "I'm actually too tired to fight with you about putting me in isolation this past week. Can I have a rain check?"

"Sure." Dylan drops an arm around my waist and helps tug me up the hill. "But just so you know, I've debated getting you one of those alarms seniors wear around their necks in case they need help. That's twice now I could've lost you."

I lay my head on his shoulder. "It's more fun to have you rescue me. Maybe next time, I'll try something a little safer. Like that stuck-in-the-shower bit Crystal does. I hear that's your specialty."

"Apparently." Dylan scoops my legs out from under me and carries me up the hill. "You'll always be my favorite damsel in distress, though."

"And you'll always be my favorite sheriff." I snuggle my face into the crook of his neck. He smells nice. Like sunshine and a light ocean breeze all mixed together.

Dylan stops walking, and Cooper does too. My dog sits and patiently waits as Dylan says, "But you're never going to stop trying to solve everyone's problems, are you?"

Guilt is eating me up inside for putting him through my near-death experiences, but I have to stand my ground. I won't change for any man.

I whisper because I haven't got much voice left, "It's in my DNA or something. I'm sorry it causes you grief sometimes."

"I know. But you don't make it easy, Sawyer. I don't know if I can survive watching you almost get killed again." He starts walking up the hill, and Cooper falls right in line.

It hurts too much to speak, or I'd tell him nothing's going to change at this point. I'm officially set in my ways.

He adds, "And by the way, if things don't work out with your uncle, you and Brittany always have a place to flop. With me."

"A place to flop?" I lean back so I can see his face. "Like two boarders paying rent?" I'm still wondering when he's going to show me the house he's building. It's weird he hasn't yet. He used to tell me everything. I can't figure what he's up to with that, because he's always up to something.

He smiles. "No rent. You could earn your keep by cooking and cleaning for me."

"What?" I punch his shoulder. "Put me down. Now!"

"What's so wrong with that?" Dylan feigns innocence as he drops my feet to the ground. "You love to cook. And I love to eat. It's a win-win if you ask me."

"If you don't know what's wrong with that, then... Forget it." I stalk up the hill. "Come on, Cooper. Let's go home." My dog gives Dylan a longing look before my pooch comes to his senses and catches up with me.

Dylan appears beside me with a twinkle in his eyes that tells me I just stepped right into one of his traps. "So if you don't want to be my tenant, what do you want to be, Sawyer?"

Ugh. It *was* one of his schemes. Why the man can't just ask a straight question when it comes to our relationship is beyond me. He plays interrogation games with me like I'm one of his suspects.

I stop and lift my chin. "If I weren't so tired...I'd..."

Dylan lays his hands on my arms. "You'd what?"

While drawing a deep breath for patience, I close my eyes. His method stinks, but he's not wrong to ask where we stand. "Okay. You win." I open my eyes and stare into his. "I know I haven't said it out loud yet, but I'd like you to be my... Partner. Boyfriend sounds too juvenile. Like we're still in high school."

"I accept." Dylan grins. "And if you want to give me a ring, I'd accept that too."

"Now you're pushing it, pal." I roll my eyes and step around him. "Dinner at Mario's tomorrow night to pay you back for your trauma is my best offer."

"You're paying? I think I'm going to like this new relationship." Dylan catches up and throws an arm around my shoulder. "I suppose I'd really be pushing it, if I asked you to refrain from investigating any future murders, though, right?"

I give him my best side-eye glance.

"Yeah. Didn't think so. Hold up a minute, please."

I stop and let my gaze meet his still-twinkling one. His apparent happiness makes me smile despite my extreme fatigue. "What? You want flowers too?"

"I'd rather have a kiss to seal the deal."

"I can do that." I stand on my tiptoes and lay one on him, taking my time and enjoying it thoroughly.

Just as I tilt my head to deepen the kiss, Brittany calls out, "Seriously? I can't even walk home in peace without having to see that?"

I chuckle and end the kiss.

Brittany shakes her head. "Come on, Cooper. Let's go before we both lose our dinner."

After they're gone, I whisper, "Brittany is something we should probably talk about."

"Not necessary. I get it. You're a package deal. One with a ton of attitude, but I'm up for the challenge." He gives me a quick kiss. "On second thought, maybe you'd better throw in those flowers."

"We'll see." I wrap my arm through his and let him walk me the rest of the way home. Just like the old days when he was my boyfriend. Hopefully, this time, things will work out a little better than the last time that ended in a failed wedding attempt. Which reminds me... "Hey, so when are you going to visit your dad and get the apology he still owes you?"

Dylan growls, "Sawyer..."

"Fine. I'll stop fixing." But only because my voice hurts too much to argue. I'll talk him into repairing that relationship as soon as I'm fully back on my feet. After that, I'm going to beat my uncle at his own game. Then, if I can get the hang of this guardian/parenting thing, I'll be a force to be reckoned with.

I guess I should thank my mom for leaving me all these challenges only she thought I could handle. Because I certainly didn't believe I could.

Watch out, Sunset Cove. Sawyer Davis is officially back, and I'm here to stay! But if we don't have another murder for a while, that'd be okay with me.

ABOUT THE AUTHOR

Tamra Baumann is an award-winning author of light-hearted contemporary romance and cozy mystery. A reality-show junkie, she justifies her addiction by telling others she's scouting for potential character material. She adamantly denies she's actually living vicariously in their closets. Tamra resides with her real-life characters—her husband, kids, and their adorable goldendoodle in the sunny Southwest. Visit her online at:

www.tamrabaumann.com

ALSO BY TAMRA BAUMANN

It Had to Be Series:

It Had to Be Him

It Had to Be Love

It Had to Be Fate

It Had to Be Them

Heartbreaker Series:

Seeing Double

Dealing Double

Crossing Double

Matchmaker Series:

Matching Mr. Right

Perfectly Ms. Matched

Matched for Love

Truly A Match

Cozy Mystery Bookshop Series:

Plotting For Murder